Praise for *Inquiry: A Districtwide Approach to Staff and Student Learning*

"The authors have provided a process of developing an inquiry learning culture for students, teachers, coaches, and principals. Writing from their own experiences, they provide specifics for planning, designing, and delivering powerful professional development."

Steve Barkley, Executive Vice President

Performance Learning Systems, Bensalem, PA

"This tidy little volume offers an ambitious lesson plan for educators who would craft in their schools a professional culture hospitable to both student and adult learning."

Roland S. Barth, Author and Founding Director

The Harvard Principals' Center, Cambridge, MA

"This book is unique because it addresses key stakeholders who inhabit the district and explains how to design systems and structures that support high quality professional development through inquiry-oriented communities."

Cathy Caro-Bruce, Educational Consultant

Wisconsin Department of Public Instruction, Madison, WI

"This book is a refreshing example of a way to actually raise student achievement by developing critical thinking skills, fostering creativity and encouraging reflective practice. I highly recommend this book to all who are interested in being a part of a school culture where all students and staff members are dedicated to achieving high levels of learning by continually improving their performance."

Michele Mattoon, Director of NSRF (National School Reform Faculty)

Harmony Education Center, Bloomington, IN

"This book identifies key obstacles in building professional learning communities, and offers productive strategies for successfully negotiating those obstacles. It will become a well-used addition to any teacher's professional library."

Laura McDermott, Principal

South Central Elementary School, Corrydon, IN

"Educators who wish to improve their own professional practice on a continual basis and who wish to support a districtwide inquiry approach that will improve student achievement and develop 21st-century thinkers should read this book."

Tiffany A. Perkins, Director of Federal Programs

Rockingham County Schools, Eden, NC

"The central precept of the book—establishing an inquiry culture for districtwide professional development that unifies the numerous piecemeal initiatives we face—really resonates for me. With inquiry as a 'golden thread' to tie together professional development, we can move from disjointed 'sit and get' sessions to true ongoing, job-embedded learning for adults, which will support coherent, meaningful learning for students."

Gail Ritchie, Instructional Coach
Fairfax County Public Schools, Centreville, VA

"This book provides essential support for all educators within every academic learning community. The authors eloquently define teacher inquiry and provide powerful instructional models and protocols that place students and their learning at the heart of what we do in education each and every day."

Jana Scott Lindsay, Educational Consultant
Saskatoon Public Schools, SK, Canada

"This text is an excellent example of a systematic and systemic approach to professional development and learning across the professional life span. I can't wait to use this text in my courses with teachers and teacher candidates as well as in my work with districts and professional development."

Jennifer Snow, Associate Professor and Chair
Boise State University, ID

"Nancy, Carol, and Sylvia have not left any stone unturned as they reveal stories of how inquiry may be embedded into the everyday practices within a district. Hearing stories from the practitioners in the schools validates the success of an inquiry approach. The unifying piece of having everyone engaged in inquiry builds a culture of learning."

Donnan Stoicovy, Lead Learner and Principal
Park Forest Elementary School, State College, PA

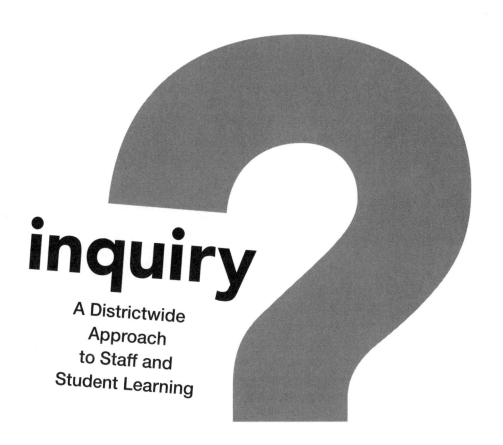

inquiry

A Districtwide
Approach
to Staff and
Student Learning

Nancy Fichtman Dana
Carol Thomas
Sylvia Boynton
Foreword by Jim Knight

A JOINT PUBLICATION

CORWIN
A SAGE Company

learningforward

CORWIN
A SAGE Company

FOR INFORMATION:

Corwin

A SAGE Company

2455 Teller Road

Thousand Oaks, California 91320

(800) 233-9936

Fax: (800) 417-2466

www.corwin.com

SAGE Ltd.

1 Oliver's Yard

55 City Road

London EC1Y 1SP

United Kingdom

SAGE India Pvt. Ltd.

B 1/I 1 Mohan Cooperative Industrial Area

Mathura Road, New Delhi 110 044

India

SAGE Asia-Pacific Pte. Ltd.

33 Pekin Street #02-01

Far East Square

Singapore 048763

Acquisitions Editor: Carol Chambers Collins
Associate Editor: Megan Bedell
Editorial Assistant: Sarah Bartlett
Production Editor: Amy Schroller
Copy Editor: Diana Breti
Typesetter: C&M Digitals (P) Ltd.
Proofreader: Charlotte J. Waisner
Indexer: Judy Hunt
Cover Designer: Scott Van Atta
Permissions Editor: Adele Hutchinson

Copyright © 2011 by Corwin

All rights reserved. When forms and sample documents are included, their use is authorized only by educators, local school sites, and/or noncommercial or nonprofit entities that have purchased the book. Except for that usage, no part of this book may be reproduced or utilized in any form or by any means, electronic or mechanical, including photocopying, recording, or by any information storage and retrieval system, without permission in writing from the publisher.

Printed in the United States of America

Library of Congress Cataloging-in-Publication Data

Dana, Nancy Fichtman, 1964-

Inquiry : a districtwide approach to staff and student learning / Nancy Fichtman Dana, Carol Thomas, Sylvia Boynton; foreword by Jim Knight.

A Joint Publication with Learning Forward

p. cm.
Includes bibliographical references and index.

ISBN 978-1-4129-9247-3 (pbk.)

1. Inquiry-based learning. 2. Teachers—In-service training. I. Thomas, Carol H. II. Boynton, Sylvia. III. Title.

LB1027.23.D36 2011
371.3—dc23   2011025900

This book is printed on acid-free paper.

11 12 13 14 15 10 9 8 7 6 5 4 3 2 1

Contents

Online resources related to *Inquiry: A Districtwide Approach to Staff and Student Learning* can be found at **http://www .corwin.com/districtwidepd.**

ONLINE RESOURCES

Resource 1. Randy's Educational Standards Relevant to Student Inquiry

Resource 2. Structure of High School Action Research Elective

Resource 3. Sample Action Research Lesson Plan

Resource 4. Inquiry Coaching Series Calendar

Resource 5. Sample Inquiry Briefs

Resource 6. Inquiry Planning Template

List of Figures

To Allen and Delores Lastinger

Through their generosity,
hundreds of educators have been touched by the power of meaningful
professional development focused on the learning of all *students.*

Foreword

Jim Knight

Far too often, professional learning in America's schools fails to have an impact on teaching practice and student learning. A major reason for this failure, as I have written in *Unmistakable Impact: A Partnership Approach for Dramatically Improving Instruction* (2010), is that educational leaders have underestimated the complexity of learning relationships between adults. I am encouraged, therefore, to see the publication of Dana, Thomas, and Boynton's *Inquiry: A Districtwide Approach to Staff and Student Learning*. The authors describe an alternative to less effective forms of professional development by grounding professional learning in a nuanced understanding of learning relationships. I describe a few of these complications below, and how the inquiry approach proposed by the authors successfully addresses them.

REFLECTION

As Thomas Davenport has explained in *Thinking for a Living* (2005), when knowledge workers such as teachers, principals, and coaches are not given the opportunity to reflect and think for themselves, they resist change. The inquiry approach described here involves identifying important questions, carefully gathering data, rigorously analyzing data, developing and implementing action plans, and sharing what has been learned. At the heart of the inquiry process is reflection, as people reflect on their questions, the data gathered, analysis, learning, and communication. When reflection is a part of learning, as it is in the inquiry process described here, educators are much more likely to embrace the experience and implement what they learn.

RELEVANCE

People are seldom motivated by professional learning experiences unless they see whatever is being learned as personally relevant. As Daniel Pink has explained in *Drive: The Surprising Truth About What Motivates Us* (2009), we are not motivated by other people's goals. Inquiry, of course, begins with people's goals as it asks participants to begin the process by posing a question, such as, "Can web 2.0 tools help my students deepen their understanding of voice in writing?" Inquiry that is not personally relevant isn't really inquiry at all, but when educators and students begin to learn about questions that matter to them, then authentic and useful learning begins.

STATUS

As Edgar Schein has explained in *Helping: How to Offer, Give, and Receive Help* (2010), we feel a conversation has been successful if we are given the status we think we deserve, unsuccessful if we are not receiving the status we think we deserve. Although Schein is talking about adult-to-adult conversations, I think his ideas apply to students. When we validate students, they often surprise us with their passion for learning.

One of the strengths of the inquiry model described by Dana, Thomas, and Boynton, in my opinion, is that it increases people's enthusiasm for professional learning by ensuring that it is largely democratic—that everyone has a choice about what they learn. When I choose my topic of inquiry, and conduct my own analysis, I am much more likely to embrace the learning than in situations where I am forced to implement someone else's ideas about good teaching.

A FOCUS ON PRACTICE

Too often professional learning in schools occurs a long way away from the classroom. If we taught swimmers the way we teach teachers, the swimmers would never get in the pool. Dana, Thomas, and Boynton, however, provide an approach to professional learning that is entirely focused on real-life application. Indeed, what the authors propose is nothing less than a culture change—shifting from training that interrupts teaching, to professional learning that is grounded in day-to-day improvements in practice.

DISTRICTWIDE

Far too frequently, professional learning—indeed learning in general—has been offered as something that is done to teachers by other leaders with little concern for districtwide or schoolwide organization and integration of learning. For example, in many settings, professional learning is given to teachers while the principal attends to other issues in a district, which means that the principal has a limited understanding of what teachers are implementing. Similarly, when professional learning is not organized and integrated across a district, coaches may be sharing a particular approach to teaching that is inconsistent with practices that are offered in district training, or that contradict those embraced by a principal. A lack of coordination across a district almost always leads to a lack of impact.

Inquiry: A Districtwide Approach to Staff and Student Learning recognizes the vital importance of districtwide coherence and provides readers with step-by-step procedures for students, teachers, principals, and coaches, as well as illustrative chapters that show the procedures in action. The authors explain what to do and then show us how it is done through many stories of inquiry in action.

Most important, Dana, Thomas, and Boynton understand that our schools will never be the places of learning our students deserve unless everyone in school is a learner. We can't expect our students to be learners, if our teachers are not learners. And we can't expect our teachers to be learners unless our principals are learners. What we need is a way to put learning at the heart of students', teachers', coaches', and administrators' work. *Inquiry: A Districtwide Approach to Staff and Student Learning* provides us with one powerful way we can do that.

Jim Knight is the Director of the Kansas Coaching Project at The University of Kansas Center for Research on Learning. He is also the author of *Instructional Coaching: A Partnership Approach to Improving Instruction* and *Unmistakable Impact: A Partnership Approach for Dramatically Improving Instruction.* Both books are published by Corwin.

Acknowledgments

One of the things that attracted us to the process of practitioner inquiry as a mechanism for educator learning and professional development was the movement's underlying respect for the knowledge generated by the people who work the closest with children every day— teachers and administrators. We are fortunate to have been inspired by numerous teacher and administrator inquirers throughout our careers, from various districts across the nation, and have learned from the knowledge they have generated from practice and the passion with which they have led classroom, school, and districtwide change and reform. In this book, we share many of these educators' inquiry endeavors to illustrate professional learning at its best. In particular, we thank Pinellas County Schools inquirers (Sharon Earle, Mike Feeney, Deanna Ferguson, Randi Latzke, Michael Morris, Michelle Morris, Rob Ovalle, Bob Poth, Art Steullet, Dorie Sundholm, Stephanie Whitaker, Monika Wolcott, Rachel Wolkenhauer); State College Area School District inquirers (Judi Kur, Marcia Heitzmann, Donnan Stoicovy); Madison-Wisconsin School District inquirers (Cathy Caro-Bruce, Jeanette Deloya, Julie Koenke); P. K. Yonge Developmental Research School inquirers (Randy Hollinger, Wendy Drexler); Collier County Schools inquirers at Village Oaks Elementary (Tracey Bowlin, Kathy Christensen, Debbie Durno, Sheila DeShields and Alicia Rosales), Fairfax County Public School Teacher inquirer (Gail Ritchie) and Union County School District inquirer (Rhonda Clyatt). According to Cochran-Smith and Lytle (2009),

> We know that much of the work of practitioner research remains radically local, generated and sustained by those who do not privilege publication and dissemination over trying to practice better, thus doing work that is consequential but invisible except to the immediate participants. (pp. 6–7)

As a result of their generosity in allowing us to publish their inquiry stories in this text, we illuminate these educators' relentless efforts to make their practice better and better for the children they teach, allowing their tremendous impact to become visible to others beyond their local vicinity.

Thank you for allowing us (and others) to learn, to grow, and to be inspired by your engagement in practitioner inquiry.

Although we have been motivated by the stories of numerous individual practitioner inquirers over the course of our careers, it was the passion for creating a systemwide program of inquiry that was ignited in the Pinellas County Schools that provided the impetus for writing this book. We thank Superintendent of Schools Julie Janssen and her Deputy Superintendent, Jim Madden, for their vision that every educator (including themselves) in Pinellas County Schools would have access to powerful professional learning opportunities through engagement in inquiry. Their endless energy to support the learning of *all* teachers, *all* administrators, and *all* students across a large school system (containing 141 schools) was critical to our work, our learning, and the writing of this book.

Large-scale, cutting edge innovation like the professional development redesign in Pinellas County Schools does not happen easily without support. We thank our colleagues at the Lastinger Center for Learning in the College of Education at the University of Florida for their contribution of resources and the very best thinking to make powerful professional development for *every* teacher focusing on the learning and achievement of *every* student a reality in school districts across our state. In particular, we thank Allen and Dolores Lastinger for endowing a center that has renewed hope for administrators, teachers, and students working in high-need, high poverty schools, as well as our Lastinger colleagues from around the state for joining with us in this exciting work, pushing our thinking and encouraging us to continue and grow in this work. Finally, we thank Lastinger Center for Learning Director Don Pemberton. The idea for this book was born on the car ride home to Gainesville, Florida, from the second annual Pinellas County Inquiry Celebration. Don not only encouraged us to write, but has been our persistent cheerleader and tirelessly supports the growth of the successful professional development endeavors described in this book. His passion for educational reform, teachers, and children is contagious, and we are grateful for all of the many opportunities he has opened up for us to share the power of inquiry with others.

As we were writing this text, we realized how challenging it was to capture and portray the complexity of an entire districtwide inquiry-oriented professional development program. In our quest to simplify and organize this multidimensional entity for the reader (and, at the same time, honor its complexity), we received tremendous assistance from our editor at Corwin, Carol Collins. We thank Carol for her great suggestions, enthusiasm for this project, and thoughtful attention to all the details.

Finally, we wish to thank our families and friends: Tom Dana, Nancy's husband, closest colleague, and best friend; Greg and Kirsten Dana, who continue to unselfishly share their mom with a computer when she sets out to write a book; David Thomas, Carol's husband, who through his love, patience, understanding, and friendship continues to show the true meaning of partners for life; Aaron Thomas, Carol's son, a collegiate athlete and scholar who provided a constant reminder of what someone can do when he is dedicated to his goals; Patti Pritz, Carol's sister, who continues to show her the meaning of courageousness and faith; Jessica and Laura Johnson, Sylvia's daughters, who are both turning into exemplary educators in their own right; and our dear friends Cathy Gould, Teresa Koehler, and Diane Yendol-Hoppey, with whom we have shared numerous years of experiences, conversation, ideas, laughter, tears, and dreams as we have grown in our love and commitment to the art of teaching and learning.

Publisher's Acknowledgments

Corwin gratefully acknowledges the contributions of the following reviewers:

Dan Cunningham, Staff Development Designer
College Board
Reston, VA

Linda Diaz, Director
Title I and Professional Development
Monroe County School District
Key West, FL

RoLesia Holman, Education Consultant
Sojourn Educational Services;
National Facilitator, San Francisco Coalition of Essential Small Schools
Cary, NC

Sue Horan
Township High School District 214
The School Reform Initiative, Illinois Center of Activity
Chicago, IL

Nancy Kellogg, Educational Consultant
Boulder, CO

Primus M. Moore, Assistant Principal
McAlester Public Schools
McAlester, OK

Terry Morganti-Fisher, Educational Consultant
Learning Forward
Austin, TX

Mary Helen Spiri, Executive Director
Chesapeake Coalition of Essential Schools
North East, MD

Sharon Tritschler, NCAC Career Academy Review Coordinator &
   National Facilitator
NSRF & NCAC
Osprey, FL

About the Authors

Nancy Fichtman Dana is currently Professor of Education in the School of Teaching and Learning at the University of Florida, Gainesville. She began her career in education as an elementary school teacher in Hannibal Central Schools, New York. Since earning her PhD from Florida State University in 1991, she has been a passionate advocate for practitioner inquiry and the promise this movement holds to enable all educators to experience powerful, job-embedded professional learning. She has coached the practitioner research of numerous educators from various districts across the nation as well as published six books and more than 50 articles in professional journals and books focused on teacher and principal professional development and practitioner inquiry. Most recently, she has worked with the Lastinger Center for Learning at University of Florida and the Pinellas County Schools to redesign professional development districtwide with inquiry at the core.

Carol Thomas most recently served as an Area Superintendent for the Pinellas County Schools. To address the needs of the nation's 24th-largest school, the district utilizes area superintendents to lead, support, and develop the work of schools. Of the 37 diverse elementary schools that Thomas oversaw, 27 made the NCLB's "adequate yearly progress" standard in 2009. For the past three years, the work of her region has been focused on a systematic approach to developing powerful instructional leaders. Using professional learning communities, principals and assistant principals studied and practiced the art of practitioner inquiry. As a result, school leaders have a clear understanding of the elements and power of an inquiry-rich environment. Her vision and leadership supports an unwavering commitment to the practice of inquiry as the cornerstone for authentic, passionate teacher/educator professional development. Thomas began her career in education as a special education teacher in Arlington, Virginia. Dr. Thomas has a PhD in Curriculum and

Instruction. Before retiring in June 2011, she dedicated 29 years to the Pinellas school community as teacher, principal, Director of Professional Development, and Assistant Superintendent of Curriculum and Instruction.

 **Sylvia Boynton** is a "professor in residence" in the University of Florida's College of Education. In this role, through the UF Lastinger Center for Learning, she works with teachers and administrators in a district-based, school improvement initiative in Pinellas County (St. Petersburg and Clearwater), Florida. She works intensively in 27 elementary schools and 12 middle and high schools with a total of 125 educators who are earning graduate degrees in the Teacher Leadership for School Improvement (TLSI) program at UF. In addition, she collaborates with five associate superintendents to provide inquiry-focused professional development to elementary principals. Most recently, she has begun working with a district/university team in an effort to infuse educator inquiry throughout all professional development. Dr. Boynton has a PhD in anthropological linguistics and an MA in Latin American Studies. She has worked in Texas and Florida as an ESL teacher.

Preface

Districtwide Professional Development: The Pieces of the Puzzle

E very district across the nation is currently focused on teacher quality and student achievement. Recent landmark federal initiatives (e.g., Race to the Top) provide financial resources to school districts, which are then charged with measuring student achievement in relation to specific learning standards. These initiatives have one element in common: the recognition that powerful professional development plays a central role in the transformation of teachers who are committed to high levels of learning and performance for all students and staff members. These resources, including the Title I Elementary and Secondary Education Act ($24.5 billion), the federal School Improvement Grants (SIG; $3.546 billion), and the competitive federal grant Race to the Top (RTTT; $4.35 billion), require school districts to design and implement a comprehensive, powerful, job-embedded professional development plan.

All school districts across the nation are held to the mandates of No Child Left Behind (NCLB) and its assurance that all students are proficient in reading and mathematics. A significant tenet of NCLB requires districts to develop, implement, and sustain a quality professional development plan in which all students and staff members are learners who continually improve their performance. By emphasizing the critical role of professional development, the federal government has signaled its belief in the importance of creating quality educators as central to improving student achievement. In addition, numerous states are involved in a federal initiative titled Differentiated Accountability (DA). This pilot program has been developed to assist states in differentiating between underperforming schools in need of dramatic interventions and those that are closer to meeting the goals of NCLB. Sixteen participating DA states (Alaska, Arkansas, Florida, Georgia, Illinois, Indiana, Louisiana, Maryland, New Jersey, New York, North Dakota, Ohio, Oklahoma, Pennsylvania, South Carolina, and Tennessee) are required to vary the intensity and type of interventions to match the academic reasons that lead to a school's identification as needing improvement. Comprehensive, systematic, professional development is a fundamental requirement of DA. DA states and districts must ensure that appropriate resources are provided to accommodate common planning time, job-embedded professional development, and professional learning communities. In addition, districts are responsible for providing technical assistance to identify job-embedded professional development and sufficient human resources to deliver a focused professional development model, including instructional coaches, lead teachers, and experts in coaching professional learning communities (PLCs). States participating in the DA pilot clearly recognize that a powerful professional development plan is critical for significant reform.

Focusing on teacher quality and student achievement through targeted professional development is an absolute necessity for districts across the nation. What is not certain is *how* to make this happen. Hence, this book was written to help districts define, develop, and implement a comprehensive, systematic approach to districtwide professional development targeted at the learning of all members of the system: adults and students alike. It is with a laser-like focus on adult and student learning simultaneously across a school district that teacher quality and student achievement can improve.

Although it is essential, the creation of a comprehensive, systematic approach to professional development that spans an entire district is a daunting and complex task, similar to putting together a very intricate and complicated jigsaw puzzle. For this reason, we use a jigsaw puzzle metaphor as an organizer for this book, to introduce components necessary to build a successful districtwide professional development program (see Figure P.1).

Figure P.1   Building a Successful Districtwide Professional Development Plan

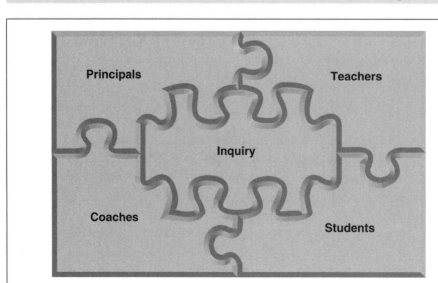

ABOUT THIS BOOK

We begin by describing the core of the puzzle: inquiry. Although there are multiple models and iterations of the inquiry process (Cochran-Smith & Lytle, 2009), in this book we discuss one model we have found to be particularly useful to both scaffold the learning of a district's adults and students and develop a productive disposition, or stance, adults and students take toward their learning. The model of inquiry we describe involves educators and students in defining questions they are passionate about exploring, collecting and analyzing data to inform their questions, and sharing what they have learned in the process with others.

Although we present inquiry as an essential and core piece of the districtwide professional development plan puzzle, we recognize that there are multiple considerations districts must take into account. In fact, there are so many things to consider that it is easy for professional development across a district to feel like an endless bombardment of current initiatives coming at principals, teachers, and students, one after another in rapid succession. We placed inquiry at the core of the puzzle to demonstrate that the many demands across district, school, and classroom roles can be tackled and unified using a similar inquiry process. Hence, our discussion of inquiry in the Introduction is not intended to cover every single component in depth. Rather, our intent is to illuminate the ways inquiry provides a healthy and productive frame for all professional development that occurs in a district, providing a sense of continuity to the many piecemeal initiatives that are often mandated by state and federal powers.

Following the Introduction, we explore each of the puzzle pieces that interlock with inquiry, one by one. Parts I, II, and III of this book focus on the important constituencies in a district that benefit from engaging in the inquiry process: principals, teachers, and students. Although it might seem more logical to begin the discussion of professional development with teachers in Part I of this book, we purposely begin with principals. We chose to focus our gaze on the administrator in Part I based on our own experiences in cultivating and studying powerful districtwide professional development across the nation (see, e.g., Dana, 2009; Dana, Tricarico, & Quinn, 2010). From our work, we have learned that it is essential for administrators to understand and buy into the inquiry process in order for powerful professional learning to unfold across a district. Because the critical role the principal plays in the process is often overlooked, we decided to begin the book with these important educators.

Following the focus on principals in Part I, teachers and students are explored in Parts II and III of the book. Because the learning of all three of these constituencies (principals, teachers, and students) is directly dependent on the coaching they receive, Part IV of this text is devoted to a discussion of the role coaches play and how to develop strong coaches across a school district.

Each Part of this book contains two chapters. In each first chapter, we define the ways the inquiry process can play out specifically with each constituency, discuss the benefits and challenges of inquiry with this particular group, and discuss a generic plan for inquiry to unfold with this constituency in a district. Another important feature included in each of these chapters is the list of selected additional resources for further reading. It would be impossible in one book to cover everything an educator needs to know about inquiry, with so many constituencies across a district. The suggested resources take the reader deeper and further into the power and process of inquiry as an approach to professional development district-twide. It takes strong facilitation to build a district culture of inquiry, and further readings and participation in training offered by such national organizations as Learning Forward, National School Reform Faculty, and Coalition of Essential Schools are suggested to help the reader successfully carry out the work described in this book.

The second chapters in Parts I through IV of this book illustrate engagement in inquiry for each constituency with real stories from districts engaging in this work. Many of these stories are derived from our work with the Lastinger Center for Learning at University of Florida. This Center partners with four large districts in our state—Collier County Public Schools, Duval County Public Schools, Miami-Dade County Public Schools, and Pinellas County Schools—to provide meaningful and powerful professional development with a particular focus on meeting the needs of teachers and administrators working in the most challenging contexts (high-need, high-poverty schools). Much of our work is in a job-embedded graduate degree program for teachers and administrators in these districts called the "Teacher Leadership for School Improvement Program." Engagement in inquiry is the signature feature of this program, and our research has revealed the power inquiry holds to unleash the potential of teachers and administrators to enact school improvement (see, e.g., Adams, Ross, Swain, Dana, Leite, & Sandbach, 2011; Ross, Adams, Bondy, Dana, Dodman, & Packer, 2010; Wolkenhauer, Boynton, & Dana, 2011). This program was named the 2011 Distinguished Program in Teacher Education by the Association of Teacher Educators.

The stories we share in the second chapters of each part of this book, based on our award-winning work with four large school districts in Florida, are included simply to help concretize the ways inquiry can play out across a district; they are not meant to be replicated in districts across the nation. Rather, we hope that these stories of challenge and success will spark your best ideas and thinking for the utility and transferability of inquiry to your own context. To enable this process, Parts I, II, III, and IV of the book end with "Questions for Discussion," to help apply what is illustrated in each part of the book to your own educational practice.

Finally, in the Conclusion to this book, we discuss the entire puzzle illustrated in Figure P.1 as a whole, highlighting what central office administrators might do to create an inquiry culture: the glue that holds all of the puzzle pieces together and leads to enhanced teacher quality and increased student achievement.

WHO IS THIS BOOK FOR?

Today's practicing professionals, whether they are based in a central office, school, or classroom, live in an era of accountability and top-down mandates that can quickly become frustrating and overwhelming. A common bond that unites central office administrators, principals, and teachers is the struggle to make sense of mandates and, at the same time, have ownership of and voice in what it takes to excel in their positions and ensure student success. This book was written for superintendents, curriculum directors, professional developers, principals, teachers at all grade levels, and professional development coaches. It is intended to help all members of a district reclaim their voices as educators in an increasingly demanding and critical education world. By developing one coherent approach to professional learning across a district, district and school-based administrators, teachers, and even students can tackle the real-world challenges and dilemmas they face every day. This book provides a roadmap for each of these constituencies to take control of their own learning.

In addition to the primary audiences for this book, school boards of education may utilize this text to develop a better understanding of the intricate nature of teaching and learning and the subsequent complexity inherent in the provision of professional development across a district. For board members, who often approve funding for professional development endeavors, this book helps to illuminate that the success of a district in meeting the needs of all of its employees and students cannot rely on a single professional development event offered once a year or the mandating of one specific training. With this knowledge, school board members can help garner support and resources for more effective and longer-lasting professional development that works.

Finally, this book is for faculty in higher education who have often suffered from the pervasive "silo effect" in education characterized by K–12 teachers isolated in classrooms (Schmoker, 2006), schools isolated in communities (Bundy, 2005; Warren, Hong, Rubin, & Uy, 2009), faculty members isolated in offices (Cox, 2004), and departments conducting insular work within their disciplines (Cox, 2004). Because of the insular nature of education entities, some colleges of education have fallen out of touch with the current needs of schools, making all colleges of education vulnerable to the growing claim that teacher education programs are to blame for problems in the field (National Council for Accreditation of Teacher Education, 2010). This book can help faculty in higher education and their students reconnect with the current needs of schools and envision a better educational system designed to constantly reinvent itself through the inquiry and action of all stakeholders: superintendents and central office administrators, principals, teachers, and students.

Whoever you are, a basic understanding of the inquiry process is essential. So, let us begin building the districtwide professional development plan puzzle from its core, with an examination of inquiry.

Introduction

Job-Embedded Learning and Inquiry for All Stakeholders

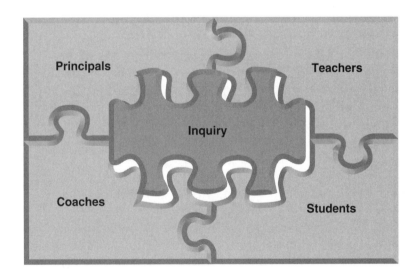

It takes a village to raise a child.

It takes a district to teach a child.

Parents know that raising a child is incredibly complex and demanding work. Because of this complexity and the demands of meeting the needs of children as they grow, responsibility for their growth and development must not lie solely with the parents but with the extended family and the community as well. Perhaps this ancient African proverb from the Igbo and Yoruba regions of Nigeria has become so popular because it rings so true: It *does* take a village to raise a child. That simple but profound statement resonates with parents everywhere.

We think our restatement and adaptation of the original proverb to the world of education—it takes a district to teach a child—will ring just as true for teachers. Teachers know that teaching is incredibly complex and demanding work. To illustrate, let's talk for a moment about what it means to be a teacher. Effective teachers must know their content deeply, know pedagogy, know human development, and know the 25 (in elementary schools) to more than 100 (in secondary schools) students they interact with each day, including identifying each one of these learners' academic, social, and emotional needs, and teachers must attend to these 25 or so individuals' needs, all unique and varied, all at the same time during each instructional moment of the day. Teachers must understand lesson planning and understand that with every lesson taught, there will be a unique outcome that results from the interaction of the context in which one teaches it, the timing of the teaching, the teacher himself or herself, and the learners in the room. Teachers must attend to management and transitions of large groups of learners before, during, and after each lesson. Teachers are bombarded with decisions each minute of their day, ranging from deciding the next steps when a planned lesson is not progressing productively to deciding whether Johnny, who just asked to use the bathroom for the third time that day, should be given permission to leave the lesson to take care of his personal needs.

In addition, teachers must constantly assess their students' learning and progress formally and informally. Teachers make contributions to the running of the school, managing such tasks as the collection of lunch money, lunch counts, bus duties, and lunch duties. They must communicate and collaborate with parents and other education professionals such as guidance counselors, the principal, school psychologists, and other teaching colleagues. In their spare time, they serve on committees, attend faculty meetings, and read professional journals and books to keep abreast of the latest developments in their field. They do all of this while simultaneously keeping an eye on high-stakes testing and their students' performance, balancing preparation for test taking and the teaching of test-taking skills with real teaching and learning of content.

Given the great complexity inherent in teaching, coupled with the numerous conversations today focused on the critical importance of raising student achievement, there is a great lesson for educators in that old African proverb. Just as raising a child must not be the sole responsibility of the parents, teaching a child and raising his or her achievement must not be the sole responsibility of an individual teacher. It really *does* take a district to teach a child.

For a district, the key to making student achievement a communal responsibility lies in enhancing teacher quality districtwide. More than a decade ago, research on this topic conducted by Linda Darling-Hammond at the Center for the Study on Teaching and Policy established the relationship between raising student achievement and teacher quality. Darling-Hammond's (1999) work examined the ways in which teacher qualifications and other school inputs were related to student achievement across states, with the findings of both the qualitative and quantitative analyses in this study suggesting that policy investments in the quality of teachers may be related to improvements in student performance:

> The findings of this study, in conjunction with a number of other studies in recent years, suggest that states interested in improving student achievement may be well advised to attend, at least in part, to the preparation and qualifications of the teachers they hire and retain in the profession. It stands to reason that student learning should be enhanced by the efforts of teachers who are more knowledgeable in their field and are skillful at teaching it to others. Substantial evidence from prior reform efforts indicates that changes in course taking, curriculum content, testing, or textbooks make little difference if teachers do not know how to use these tools well and how to diagnose their students' learning needs. (pp. 38–39)

Although the link between student achievement and teacher quality has been established for some time, districts across the nation struggle with putting into practice effective ways to enhance teacher quality and thereby harness the resources, capabilities, and energies of the entire district to teach, and reach, each individual child.

The purpose of this book is to provide districts with a comprehensive guide to building a powerful, systemwide professional development program that will enhance the quality of teachers they employ, thereby raising student achievement. Ultimately, it will help districts across the nation demonstrate the power inherent in our adaptation of the ancient proverb "It takes a village to raise a child" to "It takes a district to teach a child." In this introduction, we begin building the foundation for this program with a discussion of the latest research and thinking on teacher professional development and the power of job-embedded professional learning and inquiry.

What Is Job-Embedded Professional Learning?

Historically, the most common way that districts have provided for the professional learning of their teachers has been by holding a workshop on an inservice day, when teachers work but students have a holiday (Cochran-Smith & Lytle, 1999). Classroom teachers often refer to these days unaffectionately as "sit and get" days ("I am forced to attend this event; I sit through the day and then go back to my classroom with little support for implementing what the district has defined as important"). Administrators often refer to these days unaffectionately as "spray and pray" days ("We bring teachers together; we spray them with new knowledge, and we pray that they get something out of it"). In a similar fashion to teachers and administrators, experts in the area of teacher professional development also recognize the limitations of this traditional model. For example, leading authors and consultants in teacher professional development Joellen Killion and Cindy Harrison (2006) state,

> Traditional professional development usually occurs away from the school site, separate from classroom contexts and challenges in which teachers are expected to apply what they have learned, and often without the necessary support to facilitate transfer of learning. (p. 8)

Finally, in addition to teacher, administrator, and professional development expert testimonials, research confirms that the popular, and unfortunately still thriving, "sit and get" model of professional development, when used in isolation, is not effective in changing classroom practice (see, e.g., Desimone, 2009; Joyce & Showers, 1995).

The fact that one-day workshops in isolation are an ineffective model for teacher professional development is something that many districts know and have known about for years, but *doing* something about it is the hard part. Leading the way to resolve this age-old dilemma, Learning Forward (formerly the National Staff Development Council [NSDC]) has boldly announced sweeping changes by demanding that professional development be clearly tied to student learning. They argue that professional development must insist that "every educator engages in effective professional learning every day so every student achieves" (NSDC, 2009).

According to Learning Forward, high quality professional development is primarily conducted at the school, facilitated by well-prepared school principals and school-based coaches or other teacher leaders, and "occurs several times per week among established teams of teachers, principals, and other instructional staff members where the teams of educators engage in a continuous cycle of improvement." The emphasis is on systematic, planned, intentional, and regularly scheduled efforts to embed teacher learning within teachers' daily lives. The term that encapsulates this concept is *job-embedded professional development.* Having a district create the structures, time, and resources for all its members to engage in this important learning work is imperative to changing teaching practice to enhance teacher quality and, in turn, enhance student learning and achievement. This can be accomplished by a districtwide focus on inquiry. Inquiry becomes the golden thread that ties all professional development practice together throughout a district in meaningful and effective ways.

WHAT IS INQUIRY?

Inquiry is the systematic, intentional study of one's own professional practice (see, e.g., Cochran-Smith & Lytle, 1993, 2009; Dana & Yendol-Hoppey, 2009). Inquiring professionals seek out change by reflecting on their practice. They do this by engaging in a cyclical process of posing questions or *wonderings,* collecting data to gain insights into their wonderings, analyzing the data along with reading relevant literature, taking action to make changes in practice based on new understandings developed during inquiry, and sharing findings with others (see Figure I.1). Note that throughout this book, we

Figure I.1   Inquiry Cycle

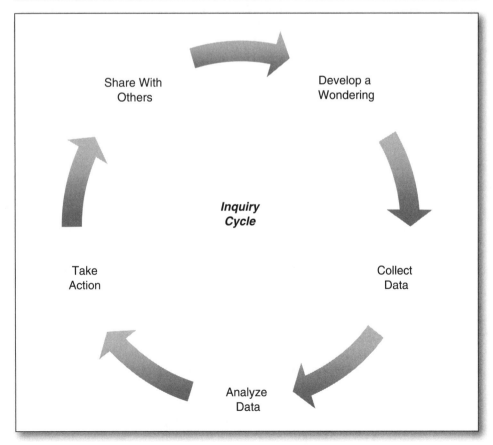

will use the terms *questions* and *wonderings* interchangeably, in reference to the topics of inquiry that educators choose to research.

Components of the Inquiry Process

The process of inquiry enables educators to tie their own learning directly to the learning of the children they teach, which is advocated as critical by Learning Forward. Let's look closely at each component of the inquiry process.

Wondering / Question Development

A wondering is a burning question an educator has about his or her practice. As explicated at the beginning of this chapter, teaching (and learning) are incredibly complex endeavors. Because of this complexity, it is natural and normal for many issues, tensions, problems, and dilemmas to emerge in classrooms and schools. Rather than sweeping them under the carpet and pretending they don't exist, educators embrace and celebrate these problems by naming them in the form of a question and making a commitment to do something about them. Wonderings can be individual, emerging from a single teacher's classroom dilemma or a single principal's desire to improve his or her administrative practice, or they can be collective, emerging from a team of teachers, administrators, or an entire school who wish to work together to improve some aspect of schooling.

Examples of individual teachers' wonderings might be "How will the facilitation of authentic learning through an online learning community in my fourth-grade classroom contribute to my students' development of positive attitudes toward learning as well as their achievement?" "How will using role play and simulations increase my students' understanding of historical events?" "What are some strategies I could utilize to facilitate better literature discussions?" Examples of individual administrators' wonderings might be "How do I use learning communities as a tool for teachers and myself in the transformation of the writing curriculum in my school?" or "What role does instituting a schoolwide meeting play in creating a caring school culture?" An example of a team or schoolwide wondering is "How do we create more culturally responsive teaching across all of the classrooms in our school, and what happens to student achievement as a result of implementing culturally responsive pedagogy?" Finally, an example of a shared, administrative team wondering might be "How can we make the district-mandated classroom walk-through process more meaningful to our work as principals?" Framing a wondering in the form of a powerful question is a critical component of the inquiry process because the question drives the quality of the work. For more information on the development of wonderings, see Chapter 2 of *The Reflective Educator's Guide to Classroom Research* (Dana & Yendol-Hoppey, 2009) and Chapter 3 of *The Reflective Educator's Guide to Professional Development* (Dana & Yendol-Hoppey, 2008).

Data Collection

Because the emphasis of job-embedded learning is on systematic, planned, intentional, and regularly scheduled efforts to embed the adult learning in a school system into teachers' and administrators' daily work, data collection is defined simply as "capturing the action that occurs in classrooms and schools." Although some of the most pervasive data in schools today include quantitative measures of student achievement, such as performance on standardized tests, progress monitoring tools, grades, and other assessment measures, data collection strategies come in many additional "flavors" as well and may include the following:

- Field notes
  - Scripting dialogue and conversation
  - Diagramming the classroom or a particular part of the classroom
  - Noting what a student or group of students are doing at particular time intervals
  - Recording what a teacher is saying
- Student work
- Documents (e.g., lesson plans, IEPs)
- Interviews
- Focus groups
- Digital pictures
- Video
- Reflective journals
- Blogs
- Surveys
- Critical friend group feedback

Given the complexity of teaching and learning, it is important for educators who engage in inquiry to collect multiple forms of data to gain insights into their wonderings. In addition, one form of data that should be an essential part of all educator inquiry is literature. Although we often don't think of literature as "data," it is a useful way to think about how the inquiry work occurring throughout a district is informed by and connected to the work of others. No district exists and operates in a vacuum. Hence, when educators inquire, their work is situated within a large, rich, preexisting knowledge base that is captured in books, journal articles, newspaper articles, conference papers, and websites. Looking at this knowledge base on teaching and learning as an existing "given" for data is important to inform practice districtwide.

Data Analysis

As a part of the inquiry process, data analysis is defined simply as creating a picture of what you have learned in relation to your wondering based on a systematic look at your data. Quantitative forms of data (data that take the form of numbers) are usually analyzed using graphs and charts that track the changes in "numbers" over time. Qualitative data (data that take the form of words) are usually analyzed in four steps.

To begin, inquirers read and reread their entire data set, with no other objective than to get a descriptive sense of what they have collected. The goal of this first step of analysis is to *describe* the inquiry data using the following questions: "What did you see as you inquired?" "What was happening?" and "What are your initial insights into the data?" The description step may be accomplished by talking it through with other educators, writing it out, or choosing a combined approach and taking detailed notes.

Next, inquirers begin the *sense-making* step by reading their entire data set and asking questions such as, "What sorts of things are happening in my data?" "What do I notice?" "How might different pieces of my data fit together?" and "What pieces of my data stand out from the rest?" The answers to these questions begin the process of grouping or sorting data by theme, category, pattern, or some other organizing unit. Sometimes inquirers get stuck in the sense-making stage and need some prompts to help begin this sense-making process. Figure I.2 offers some organizing units that can serve as prompts during this phase of the analysis. To decide on organizing units, educators may take notes in the margins of their data. Data may be physically cut apart and placed in discrete piles or categories. Still another strategy to use during this step is to group data by using a different color marker for each theme or pattern identified and to highlight excerpts of data that fit different patterns.

Figure I.2   Examples of Organizing Units

Examples of Organizing Units		
Chronology	Key events	Various settings
People	Processes	Behaviors
Issues	Relationships	Groups
Styles	Changes	Meanings
Practices	Strategies	Episodes
Encounters	Roles	Feelings

The third step of the qualitative analysis process is *interpretation.* In this step, statements that express what was learned and what that learning means are constructed by looking at the patterns that were coded and asking and answering questions such as, "What was my initial wondering and how do these patterns inform it?" "What is happening in each pattern and across patterns?" and "How are these happenings connected to teaching? To students? To the subject matter and the curriculum? To the classroom or school context?"

The findings from this step can be illustrated in a number of ways, including but not limited to the following: themes, patterns, categories, metaphors, similes, claims/assertions, typologies, and vignettes. Figure I.3 outlines possible illustrative techniques and provides examples from teachers' inquiry. These strategies help illustrate, organize, and communicate inquiry findings to an audience after the fourth step (*implications*) is completed by answering such questions as: (1) "What have I learned about myself as a teacher/administrator?," (2) "What have I learned about students?," (3) "What have I learned about the larger context of schools and schooling?," (4) "What are the implications of what I have learned for my teaching/administrative practice?," (5) "What changes might I make in my practice?," and (6) "What new wonderings do I have?"

Figure I.3   Strategies for Illustrating Your Findings

Theme/Pattern/Category/Label/Naming—A composite of traits or features; a topic for discourse or discussion; a specifically defined division; a descriptive term; set apart from others.

   Examples: collaboration, ownership, care, growth

Metaphor—A direct comparison between two or more seemingly unrelated subjects, in order to suggest a similarity.

   Example: Central administration is the glue that holds a professional development program together.

Simile—A comparison of two unlike things, usually using the word "like" or "as."

   Example: Creating a districtwide professional development program is like putting together an intricate jigsaw puzzle.

Claim/Assertion—A statement of fact or assertion of truth.

   Example: Inappropriate expectations discouraged many of the learners in my classroom and hindered my effectiveness as a writing teacher.

Typology—A systematic classification of types

   Example: Different uses for puppets—instructional, entertainment, therapeutic

Vignette—A brief descriptive literary sketch

   Example: The Struggle for Power: Who Is in Control?

   The children were engaged in conversation at the meetings, jobs were continuing to get done, but there was still a struggle centering around who was in control. With the way the class decided to make a list of jobs, break the jobs up into groups, choose the people they wanted to work with, there were breaks in communication. Conflicts were arising with the groups. Everyone was mostly aiming to get "their own" way.

Taking Action and Sharing Learning With Others

Once data are analyzed, educators take action based on what they learned through the process and share their learning with others. Sharing can be accomplished in faculty meetings, grade-level meetings, publications, blogging, conferences, and/or districtwide inquiry showcases. Figure I.4 illustrates one page from a districtwide inquiry showcase event in Pinellas County Schools in Florida. Regardless of the venue in which work is shared, sharing is important for a number of reasons. First, the process of preparing findings to share with others helps all educators to clarify their thinking about their work. In addition to clarifying their thinking, they give other professionals access to their thinking and the opportunity to question, discuss, debate, and relate. This process helps educators and their colleagues push and extend their thinking about practice as well.

Figure I.4   Districtwide Inquiry Showcase Program

Third Annual Inquiry Celebration

Pinellas County Schools/University of Florida Lastinger Center for Learning

May 6, 2010

Reading Confidence: Under Construction

How will conferencing in reading affect an individual student's lexile and comprehension success on reading assessments?

Brenda Bauerlein, VE Resource Teacher K–5/Read180 Teacher
Blanton Elementary

This fourth-grade student has an apparent stumbling block when she takes a reading assessment on the computer or on paper. Will individual reading conferences increase this student's success in reading assessment scores and reading lexile? Data from the classroom assessments, FAIR (Florida Assessments for Instruction in Reading), SRI assessments, state assessments, and reading conference notes will be analyzed.

Adult Modeling of Independent Reading

What would be the effect of modeling independent reading on students' attitudes toward reading?

Suzanne Shirk, Library and Information Specialist
74th Street Elementary

What would be the effect of modeling independent reading on students' attitudes toward reading? We are always telling our students to read, read, read . . . but do they ever see us reading? I wonder if they see an adult reading and on a consistent basis, would the kids notice, and how would it affect their attitudes toward reading?

Pinellas Vocabulary Project

How does Pinellas Vocabulary Project impact student vocabulary knowledge over time?

Dana Robinson, Reading/Literacy Coach
74th Street Elementary

As the reading coach at my school, I was presented with the Pinellas Vocabulary Project to implement in my school with teachers and students. This was a new way to work, and I wondered whether it would actually improve student vocabulary knowledge over time. Would students retain the new vocabulary words using this new way of instruction?

A Challenge for Change Agents

How can we apply change agent strategies to move teachers forward in their use of the readers' workshop model?

Alisa Gatlin, Principal, and Karen Aspen, Assistant Principal
Forest Lakes Elementary

A real change in the professional development paradigm was evident when we learned that a literacy professional development coach was assigned to our school for one week every month for the year. Teacher responses to the news ran the gamut. Our challenge was to develop a plan that allows us to get the best possible results from this valuable resource.

Clarifying, pushing, and extending thinking are not the only benefits of sharing. Fellow professionals also benefit from the knowledge colleagues create through engagement in the inquiry process.

Although the individual steps in the inquiry process just described in this section (formulating a question/wondering, collecting data, analyzing data, taking action, and sharing with others) are important, the ultimate goal of engaging in the process is to create an inquiry stance toward teaching. This stance becomes a professional positioning, where questioning one's own practice becomes part of an educator's work and eventually a part of the district culture. According to distinguished educational scholars Marilyn Cochran-Smith and Susan Lytle (2001),

> a legitimate and essential purpose of professional development is the development of an inquiry stance on teaching that is critical and transformative, a stance linked not only to high standards for the learning of all students but also to social change and social justice and to the individual and collective professional growth of teachers. (p. 46)

By cultivating this inquiry stance toward teaching, teachers and administrators play a critical role in enhancing their own professional growth. As a result, teacher (and administrator) quality is enhanced, with the ultimate beneficiaries being students.

Now that we have provided a brief overview of the inquiry process, you are probably recognizing the ways engagement in the process of inquiry is closely related to some current and popular district initiatives such as professional learning communities, lesson study, and response to intervention. Let's look more closely at these connections, recognizing that these are only a few of many.

What Is the Relationship Between Inquiry and Professional Learning Communities?

Professional learning communities (PLCs) are defined generically as small groups of faculty and/or administrators who meet regularly to study more effective learning and teaching practices (Dana & Yendol-Hoppey, 2008). A PLC's time together is often structured by the use of protocols to ensure focused, deliberate conversation and dialogue about student work and student learning. Joseph McDonald and his colleagues explain the importance of utilizing protocols:

> In diplomacy, protocol governs who greets whom first when the President and Prime Minister meet, and other such matters. In technology, protocols enable machines to "talk" with one another by precisely defining the language they use. In science and medicine, protocols are regimens that ensure faithful replication of an experiment or treatment; they tell the scientist or doctor to do this first, then that, and so on. And in social science, they are the scripted questions that an interviewer covers, or the template for an observation. But in the professional education of educators? One could argue that elaborate etiquette, communicative precision, faithful replication, and scripts would prove counterproductive here. Don't we best learn from each other by just talking with each other? No, we claim. Among educators especially, *just* talking may not be enough. The kind of talking needed to educate ourselves cannot rise spontaneously and unaided from *just* talking. It needs to be carefully planned and scaffolded. (McDonald, Mohr, Dichter, & McDonald, 2003, p. 4)

Protocols for educators provide a script or series of timed steps for how a conversation among professionals on a chosen topic will develop.

A variety of different protocols have been developed for use in PLCs by a number of noteworthy organizations, such as Learning Forward (see, e.g., Lois Brown Easton's [2004] *Powerful Designs for Professional Learning*), the Southern Maine Partnership (see, e.g., http://usm.maine.edu/smp/about/index), and the National School Reform Faculty (NSRF), who developed the version of a professional learning community called Critical Friends Groups (CFGs). Further information about NSRF and access to their protocols can be found at www.nsrfharmony.org. The CFGs provide deliberate time and structures dedicated to promoting adult professional growth that is directly linked to student learning. When used in a PLC, protocols ensure planned, intentional conversation by teachers about student work, a teacher's dilemma, a lesson to be taught, or other aspects of practice. Different protocols are selected for use depending upon the topic for discussion that day. Practice in matching protocols to particular purposes and uses in meetings is part of the NSRF training. We highly recommend training by NSRF or similar organizations (such as Coalition of Essential Schools or Learning Forward) to develop the skill set necessary to effectively select and facilitate protocols in professional settings.

Inquiry and PLCs as mechanisms for teacher professional growth have a lot in common. For example, inquiry is defined as *systematic, intentional* study by educators of their own practice, and protocols *systematize* conversation that occurs between educators to *intentionally* focus their dialogue on students and their learning during professional learning community meetings. Hence, inquiry and PLCs can be intricately intertwined with one another. In essence, inquiry is the process that PLCs can utilize to focus their work during an entire school year. Simply put, PLCs can serve as powerful "containers" for the process of inquiry to unfold in various configurations districtwide.

WHAT IS THE RELATIONSHIP BETWEEN INQUIRY AND RESPONSE TO INTERVENTION?

Another approach that shares similarities with inquiry and is receiving current attention from educators across the United States is response to intervention (RTI). RTI is an intervention approach that is a part of the eligibility process for Emotional Behavior Disorders (EBD) and Specific Learning Disabilities (SLD), and this process is strongly supported by both the Individuals With Disabilities Education Act (IDEA) and No Child Left Behind (NCLB). However, the application of RTI is much broader than a screening process to determine special education eligibility. The goal of RTI is to prevent unnecessary student assignment to special education by offering low-performing students intense, individualized academic intervention paired with systematic study of the intervention. According to Jim Wright (n.d.), a school psychologist and administrator from central New York, RTI gives a student with delays one or more research-validated interventions. As the intervention is used, the student's learning is systematically studied or monitored to identify whether the interventions will enable the student to catch up with his or her peers.

The RTI process follows the inquiry process described in this book as the intervention is systematically studied. The process begins with problem analysis that identifies the desired change for the student experiencing academic or behavioral difficulty. Next, educators design and implement an evidence-based intervention. Finally, the effectiveness of the intervention is determined by synthesizing and analyzing the data collected. This step is termed *response to intervention* because during this step a student's or group of students' response to the implemented intervention is measured to evaluate the effectiveness of the instruction. Just as inquiry focuses on the systematic and intentional collection of data about a wondering, in RTI, educators focus on systematically and intentionally collecting data to understand whether the response to the intervention results in adequate academic and/or behavioral growth. According to Jim Wright (n.d.), to implement RTI effectively,

> schools must develop a specialized set of tools and competencies, including a structured format for problem solving, knowledge of a range of scientifically based interventions that address common reasons for school failure, and the ability to use various methods of assessment to monitor student progress in academic and behavioral areas.

Given the sophistication that educators need to possess in each step of the inquiry process, as well as the importance of adequate knowledge of powerful interventions, the success of RTI will likely depend on whether the process is appropriately implemented and whether an inquiry stance is embraced by highly skilled professionals. The inquiry process illustrated in this book can offer support to those engaged in RTI. In fact, RTI can become one form of inquiry occurring in a district.

What Is the Relationship Between Inquiry and Lesson Study?

Inquiry is often tied directly to curriculum and the implementation of curriculum. When curriculum and its implementation is the focus of inquiry, inquiry shares all of the same core features of the popular professional development strategy termed *lesson study*. As a professional development strategy, lesson study enables teachers to systematically and collaboratively examine and improve their teaching practice by "studying" lessons. Teachers create study lessons together by planning, teaching, observing, critiquing, and revising the lessons as a group. This spiraling process is driven by an overarching goal and a research question shaped by the group, in the same way inquiry is shaped by a wondering. The end result is not only a better developed lesson, but typically teachers also develop a stronger understanding of the content, enhanced observation skills, stronger collegial networks, and a tighter connection between daily practice and long-term goals (Lewis, Perry, & Hurd, 2004). The lesson study typically culminates with a report that summarizes what the study taught them, similar to the way inquiry culminates with sharing the work with others. In essence, lesson study becomes a specialized form of the inquiry process focused on the planning and teaching of one lesson and the ways that lesson plays out for multiple teachers and learners in a school or in multiple schools in a district. Like RTI, lesson study can become one form of inquiry occurring in a district.

WHAT MIGHT A STRUCTURE FOR CREATING A DISTRICTWIDE PROGRAM OF INQUIRY LOOK LIKE?

We just looked at the ways the process of inquiry (formulating a question/ wondering, collecting data, analyzing data, taking action, and sharing with others) is related to three common initiatives districts are engaged in throughout the nation: professional learning communities, response to intervention, and lesson study. Sometimes, teachers and administrators feel overwhelmed by the number of initiatives a district takes on. They are required to take a string of seemingly unrelated workshops, and then they are expected to do something about the initiatives in their own schools and classrooms. This is why many well-intentioned initiatives never quite actualize their potential for improving instruction and enhancing schooling for all learners.

Yet, by drawing connections between the process of inquiry and initiatives such as learning communities, response to intervention, and lesson study, we set the stage for the premise of this book: Engagement in inquiry is a powerful overarching framework that can change district professional development for teachers and administrators from an unsystematic series of events to the natural and normal way a district does business every day. In casting inquiry as the golden thread that ties all professional development together throughout a district, every educator in the district is engaged every day in learning that is directly related to students and their learning. The result is the enhancement of teacher quality and student achievement districtwide.

So how can an entire system, such as a school district, make inquiry a core component of its daily work? The answer lies in creating multiple opportunities (and incentives) for all members of the district to engage in the process at various times, in various places, and in various configurations. At the district level, principals meet and support one another in studying their own administrative practice. At the school level, teachers meet and support each other in studying students and their learning. At the classroom level, inquiry as a pedagogy is instituted with students to unleash their learning potential.

We'll spend the remainder of this book exploring the ways districts can create the structures to support administrators (Part I), teachers (Part II), and students (Part III) in the work of inquiry. In addition, we'll explore the important role coaches can play in the development of a districtwide program of inquiry (Part IV). Finally, in the Conclusion to this book, we'll focus on district leadership (the superintendent and other central office administrators) and the ways these professionals can create and sustain a culture of inquiry for *all* who work in the district—the adults and the children—to thrive! Before we begin an in-depth look at each component of the districtwide structure, we end this Introduction with a true story of the ways engagement in a districtwide program of inquiry can impact student learning and achievement and a few resources we recommend for learning more about the power of job-embedded learning and the process of inquiry.

HOW ENGAGEMENT IN A DISTRICTWIDE PROGRAM OF INQUIRY CAN IMPACT STUDENT LEARNING AND ACHIEVEMENT

Educators in Pinellas County Schools in Florida worked on developing and implementing a structure for creating a districtwide program of inquiry, with exciting results. To illustrate, we turn to the story of four elementary schools in Pinellas County that service high-need, high-poverty areas of the district. In the fall of 2008, these four elementary schools confronted the harsh reality of their state assessment scores. In Florida, schools are assigned a "grade" based on students' achievement on these tests. What the staff at each of these buildings was struggling with was an overall score of a "C," precariously close to a "D" ranking. To make matters worse, if the overall writing scores of the fourth graders at these schools did not increase on the following year's writing assessment, these schools would sink deeper into the federal sanctions.

Fortunately for these schools, their administrative team had spent an entire year studying the inquiry process, with each principal and assistant principal not only studying the process but also engaged in his or her own inquiry project. Each principal rallied a group of teachers at his or her school, explained his or her positive experience with inquiry, and suggested tackling the dilemma of their school grade and writing scores by using inquiry. Teachers met regularly to wonder, "what if," question, and research ways to better instruct students in the writing process.

With the coaching support of the school-based administrators, literacy coaches, and district administrators, wonderings emerged and groups of teachers at the four buildings began their first experience with the inquiry process. Initial action research questions focused on the use of explicit instruction in the writing process, the use of flexible diagnostic grouping for writing instruction, the implementation of differentiated writing homework, and additional intensive instruction for the most struggling students. Teachers in all four schools met to review the data that was generated as a result of action steps that addressed their wondering. Student work, teachers' reflections, and administrator walk-through observations were the data sources these teachers drew upon to analyze, catalog, and continually revise their action steps throughout the school year.

Fast forward to the end of the school year, when all four schools were excited to participate in a districtwide celebration of inquiry and present their work to other professionals. Just as the teachers and administrators were on their way to the district inquiry celebration, they received the results of the state writing assessment completed in February of that school year, during the heart of their inquiry work focused on writing. The writing scores on the state assessment at all four schools showed dramatic improvement. Each fourth grade demonstrated a minimum growth of 10 percentage points in their writing scores, with one school posting a score of 90% proficiency (up from the previous year's score of 63%). However, the most impressive was the school that moved from 51% of their students proficient in writing to a whopping 92% proficiency! As if this wasn't enough to celebrate, as the school year came to a close, all four schools had replaced their overall "C" school grade with an "A"!

Not only had the academic scores soared, so had these teachers' and administrators' attitudes and passion to study their practice. In the midst of sharing their inquiry projects with others, these teachers and school leaders were already wondering, planning, questioning, and "what if-ing" for the next school year.

WHERE CAN I LEARN MORE ABOUT JOB-EMBEDDED PROFESSIONAL LEARNING AND INQUIRY?

To create a ripe context to allow the process of inquiry to unfold in your district, we suggest beginning by deepening your knowledge of powerful professional development, job-embedded learning, and the process of inquiry in general. The following are additional resources to accomplish these goals:

• Learning Forward (http://www.learningforward.org). Explore their website and learn more about this outstanding organization that advocates for job-embedded learning.

• Yendol-Hoppey, D., & Dana, N. F. (2010). *Powerful professional development: Building expertise within the four walls of your school.* Thousand Oaks, CA: Corwin. This book supplements the notion of job-embedded professional development introduced in this chapter by providing a more in-depth look at the concept. In addition, this text provides a number of tools for actualizing job-embedded learning in addition to inquiry.

- Dana, N. F., & Yendol-Hoppey, D. (2009). *The reflective educator's guide to classroom research: Learning to teach and teaching to learn through practitioner inquiry.* This book explicates each step of the inquiry process (wondering development, data collection, data analysis, action, and sharing) in much greater detail than the descriptions found in this chapter.

REVIEW AND LOOKING AHEAD

In this Introduction, we presented the concept of job-embedded learning as a mechanism to provide powerful professional development for all members of a school district. Specifically, we

1. named practitioner inquiry as the golden thread that ties all professional development together throughout a district in meaningful and effective ways—the first piece of the districtwide professional development plan puzzle;

2. defined inquiry and examined each component of the inquiry process in depth (developing a wondering, data collection, data analysis, taking action, and sharing learning with others);

3. explored the relationships between inquiry and three current and popular district initiatives: learning communities, RTI, and lesson study; and

4. introduced a structure for creating a program of inquiry and illustrated the ways engagement in inquiry links directly to student achievement with the story of four elementary schools in the district where we work: Pinellas County Schools.

In Part I of this book, we continue to build our districtwide professional development plan puzzle by focusing our gaze on one particular constituency in the district—the administrators—and explore the ways inquiry can play out powerfully for this special and important group of educators.

PART I

The Administrator's Role

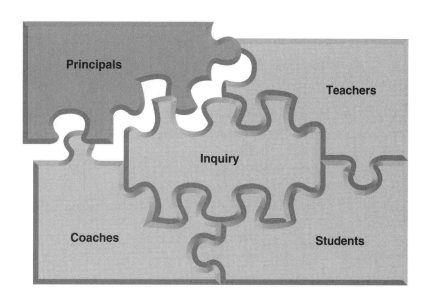

The Principal Professional Learning Community

Principal inquiry is a process that allows me to do three things I need and like to do but rarely make time for: be a reflective practitioner, work with a true professional learning community, and model instructional leadership.

—Mike Delucas, Principal, Williston High School

Building a successful, powerful, systemwide professional development program must begin with a focus on administration. In order for teachers to experience powerful professional development at the building level, principals must understand and know what powerful job-embedded learning through inquiry looks and feels like. Yet, according to Roland Barth (2001),

> Professional development for principals has been described as a "wasteland." Principals take assorted courses at universities, attend episodic inservice activities within their school systems, and struggle to elevate professional literature to the top of the pile of papers on their desks. (p. 156)

Barth (2001) calls for districts to shift the ways they conceptualize principal professional development from answering the questions,

"What should principals know and be able to do?" and "How can we get them to know and do it?" to "Under what conditions will school principals become committed, sustained, lifelong learners in their important work" (p. 157)? Building on the work of Roland Barth, this chapter introduces the cross-district principal professional learning community (PPLC) as a mechanism to support principals in becoming committed, sustained, lifelong learners.

What Is a PPLC?

A PPLC is a small group of principals from across the district (typically about 5–10 people) who meet on a regular basis (usually as part of the district's regularly scheduled administrative team meetings) to learn from practice through structured dialogue and engagement in continuous cycles of inquiry (articulating a wondering, collecting data to gain insights into the wondering, analyzing data, making improvements in practice based on what was learned, and sharing learning with others). PPLCs are an effective way for principals to reflect on their practice, set personal and school goals, develop a plan to achieve those goals, assess progress, and continue to grow professionally throughout their careers, all with the support of other professionals along the way.

There are two equally powerful ways the PPLC can function. First, a group of principals might share a common passion or dilemma about their practice as administrators and articulate and explore one collective wondering together.

> A group of principals Carol and Sylvia worked with were frustrated with the way the classroom walk-through was playing out in their schools. Although they were going through all the motions of the classroom walk-through as they were taught to do during a districtwide inservice, this group of principals lamented that they, as well as their teachers, found little meaning in the process. They made a mutual commitment to formulate a learning community and work together to make the process of observation more meaningful to their work as administrators as well as for the teachers in their buildings. Together, they crafted one collective wondering that guided their inquiry: In what ways will focusing our classroom walk throughs on teacher-selected growth areas improve the walk-through process for us as administrators as well as for our teachers? Over several months, they worked together to create a plan to modify and enrich the classroom walk-through model. Their plan was informed by the literature on classroom walk throughs and teacher professional development, as well as data they collected at their school sites related to the ways teachers experienced the current classroom walk-through process. Sharing and discussing their data at learning community meetings led to

further refinement and revision of the walk-through process for implementation the following school year, resulting in a much more effective implementation of the classroom walk-through in the eyes of the principals and their teachers.

Although principals often share a common dilemma they wish to explore (like making the classroom walk-through more meaningful and useful, as described above), frequently a principal faces complex issues specific to his or her school. Across a district, each principal functions within his or her own unique setting, serving diverse student populations and providing instructional leadership for faculties of teachers who vary in their teaching styles and personalities. Because of this variety, a principal may have burning individual questions that are critically important to that principal's practice.

Hence, the second way a PPLC can function is as a sounding board in which each principal in the group can explore his or her own inquiry question. In this setting, the PPLC supports each principal through individual inquiry projects.

Nancy facilitated the work of a group of five principals from elementary, middle, and high schools in the same learning community. Each principal defined his or her own wondering to explore, and the group met about once a month to help each other develop their individual wonderings, develop a plan to collect data to gain insights into those wonderings, talk about how data collection was going, help each other analyze data once it was collected, and support each other in "packaging" their individual learning to share with others. The individual wonderings explored by this group of principals were as follows:

- What effect does the inclusion environment have on the reading achievement of eighth-grade language arts students at Lake Butler Middle School?
- In what ways will implementing the continuous improvement model help increase student achievement at my elementary school?
- In what ways are out-of-school or in-school suspensions as a consequence for discipline referrals affecting student performance?
- What actions can our faculty take to improve the reading achievement of our lowest quartile students?
- How does my teachers' implementation of a purchased educational computer program relate to student learning?

The principals in this PPLC reported how much they learned not only from their own inquiries, but from the inquiries of their colleagues (Dana et al., 2010).

Regardless of the ways a PPLC functions (one collective wondering explored together as a group or each principal exploring individual wonderings and providing support for one another in their individual explorations), it is critical for the PPLC to define powerful questions to explore. The power of learning that occurs through the inquiry process can only be as good as the initial questions that frame the entire inquiry journey. Usually principal wonderings emerge from one of nine different passions central to the effective functioning of a school: professional development, curriculum development, individual teachers, individual students, school culture/community, leadership, management, school performance, or social justice. Figure 1.1 contains 50 examples of principal wonderings by passion.

Figure 1.1   50 Examples of Principal Wonderings by Passion

Passion	Sample Questions
Professional Development	In what ways will focusing our classroom walk throughs on teacher-selected growth areas improve the walk-through process for us as administrators as well as for our teachers?
	How does the process of peer coaching help veteran teachers continue to learn and grow, and what role can the principal play in facilitating this process?
	In what ways can I, as a principal, help facilitate the professional growth of the teachers in my building through engagement in action research?
	How can I, as an administrator, use formal and informal assessments to effectively coach differentiated instruction plans with my reading teachers?
	How do I balance my role in ensuring that teachers work effectively in their PLCs with encouraging teachers to develop greater professional autonomy?
Curriculum Development	In what ways does a cross-school curriculum project impact student learning and our school community?
	How can we become proficient at evaluating the achievement growth of students during their independent reading?
	How can a science homework structure that was developed, implemented, and monitored by the principal and assistant principal affect student achievement and attitudes in science?
	What can I do to ensure that the level of student talk is maturing to a high level of thinking and conversing?
	How can I build my own knowledge of exemplary writing practice?
	How do I use learning communities as a tool for teachers and myself to utilize in the transformation of the writing curriculum at our school?

Passion	Sample Questions
Individual Teachers	What types of support will help my new teachers succeed?
	How can I best help an out-of-field teacher?
	How can I work with a struggling teacher to help her learn to use student writings to evaluate their process and guide her instruction?
	How can I support a novice literacy coach as she learns to model effective instruction for teachers who may feel threatened by her sophistication?
	How do I connect the non-core teachers (art, music, P.E.) to the grade-level PLCs so that together all teachers are supporting the same instructional goals?
	What is the relationship between changing a veteran teacher's grade level assignment and getting her out of a rut?
Individual Students	What happens to struggling readers in our school after they leave intervention programs?
	What effect does the inclusion environment have on the reading achievement of eighth-grade Language Arts students at Lake Butler Middle School?
	If the principal and assistant principal use the identified, explicit vocabulary that parallels the classroom vocabulary instruction during their daily interactions with students, how would it impact the vocabulary acquisition of primary ESOL students?
	How does providing "just right" literature to gifted readers change their attitudes about reading?
	How can my conferring with struggling students once a week during their lunch period help these students make math connections between isolated math skills and their day-to-day encounters?
	What is the relationship between students' participation in Williston High's SWAS (School Within A School) Credit Retrieval Program and their success in high school?
Community/ Culture Building	What role does a weekly schoolwide meeting play in creating a caring school culture?
	In what ways can our school develop a collaborative culture characterized by teachers from different grade levels communicating, understanding, and sharing expectations for all of our students?
	How does the development and implementation of a Behavior Support Team affect school culture?
	How would an increase in social conversations between administration and staff, coupled with recognition of teacher effort, affect staff morale and the teachers' willingness to implement new ideas?
	What would be the impact on school culture of the principal and assistant principal covering individual teacher's classes, to enable those teachers to observe in other teachers' classrooms?

(Continued)

Figure 1.1 (Continued)

Passion	Sample Questions
Leadership Skills	What do I learn from comparing and contrasting my own perceptions, my teachers' perceptions, my leadership team's perceptions, and my supervisor's perceptions about my instructional leadership as a principal?
	How can I develop a system to capture information about the teachers in my school as I confer with them and observe their teaching practices that will help me assess their strengths and growth areas?
	How does implementing a semi-departmentalized instructional model in an elementary school impact both student achievement and teacher effectiveness?
	How will using protocols (see NSRFharmony.org) during staff meetings and PLCs affect the instructional practices of teachers at my school?
	How do I improve my ability to inspire others to achieve a common purpose?
	How do I build a cohesive and spirited team?
	How can I, as an administrator, promote teacher leadership at my school?
Management	What are teachers' levels of satisfaction with the current block schedule?
	How could I provide additional reading instructional time for the intermediate grade teachers in order to accelerate student growth?
	How could I use the human resources currently available to our school (i.e., specialists within the school, student peers, cross-age tutors, high school students, parent volunteers, business partnerships, etc.) to provide more in-depth reading instruction?
	How can we all work together (students, teachers, lunch paraprofessionals, kitchen workers, custodians, and principal) to make lunchtime a cooperative and pleasant time for everyone?
School Performance	In what ways will implementing the continuous improvement model help increase student achievement at my school?
	What actions can our faculty take to improve the reading achievement of our lowest quartile students?
	If our school develops a process to better understand how student writing looks different from grade to grade and develops systems to identify expected growth in each genre at each grade, what would be the impact on student writing?
	How can I support teachers in becoming really good at using Independent Reading Logs to evaluate students' growth in reading?
	How does the principal's or assistant principal's explicit, planned recognition of student homework affect student attitude and achievement?

Passion	Sample Questions
Social Justice	How do service learning projects influence the development of student character?
	What is the effect of structured class meetings on the interpersonal relations between students and between teacher and student?
	What would be the effects of visual reminders on the use of kind and respectful words in our school?
	In this era of holding teachers directly accountable for student performance, how can I help teachers see that cultural variations among their students can be academic assets?
	What can we do to help close the achievement gap and improve our practice with African American students?

WHAT ARE THE BENEFITS OF PPLCS?

In addition to providing principals with a meaningful way to grow professionally, PPLCs provide other benefits to principals and their schools. There have been numerous discussions in the literature about teacher isolation that depict teaching as a lonely profession in which teachers close their classroom doors and have little interaction with other teachers in their buildings (see, e.g., Flinder, 1988; Lieberman & Miller, 1992; Lortie, 1975; Smith & Scott, 1990). If teaching is isolated, so too is the principalship.

> Principals, just like teachers, need and treasure collegiality and peer support. Yet, perhaps even more than teachers, principals live in a world of isolation. Just as there is often distance for teachers between their adjoining classrooms, the distance across the district to another school is even greater. When principals associate with peers, it is often at an administrators' meeting. In these infrequent and somewhat formal meetings, principals often feel that it is negatively stigmatized for them to admit to their peers that they do "not know" something. Neither the time nor the setting is conducive to collegial support or to the exchange of ideas and concerns. (Barth, 1990, p. 83)

In contrast, PPLCs provide an ideal setting for collegial support and the free exchange of ideas and concerns, taking principals out of isolation and into collaboration.

A second important benefit of PPLC work is that by engaging in this process, principals become role models for the teachers and students in their building. According to Roland Barth (1990), a precondition for realizing the extraordinary potential principals have to improve their schools is for them to become head learners.

Perhaps the most powerful reason for principals to be learners as well as leaders, to overcome the many impediments to their learning, is the extraordinary influence of modeling behavior. Do as I do, as well as I say, is a winning formula. If principals want students and teachers to take learning seriously, if they are interested in building a community of learners, they must not only be head teachers, headmasters, or instructional leaders. They must, above all, be head learners. I believe it was Ralph Waldo Emerson who once said that what you do speaks so loudly that no one can hear what you say. (p. 72)

Principal professional learning communities enable all principals across a district to become communities of head learners and do the important professional learning they advocate for their teachers, thereby modeling learning for teachers (and subsequently, students). On a related note, by engaging in PPLC work, principals experience what powerful, collaborative professional learning feels like, perhaps for one of the first times in their own careers as educators. Experiencing powerful, collaborative professional learning makes principals more likely and able to create the space and opportunity for meaningful, job-embedded, collaborative learning to occur among their teachers.

> To illustrate, we turn to the three years of inquiry work of Monika Wolcott, an elementary school principal Carol and Sylvia worked with in Pinellas County Schools, Florida. During a recent annual districtwide inquiry celebration, where educators came together to share the results of their year-long research, Monika and several of her principal colleagues presented a collaborative group inquiry. Monika talked about the impact of inquiry on their collective learning.

>> Without my colleagues and fellow principals I would have given up on my inquiry. I realized that being confused and not having the answers was just part of the process of studying my work. The best part of making sense of our inquiry work was that it wasn't just my work but our work. We became totally relaxed and open to saying, "I'm not sure" or "I don't know how to analyze this data." When we realized we didn't have to be right and learning meant making mistakes, our minds opened to all sorts of possibilities and our conversations shifted from complaints and barriers to positive solutions to our dilemmas and what we could do together. We realized how powerful this type of learning was for us and imagined how we could create the context as principals in our own schools for this type of learning to occur among our teachers.... Professional development at its best! (M. Wolcott, personal communication, May, 2010)

WHAT ARE THE CHALLENGES OF PPLC WORK?

At this point in the chapter, we would not be surprised if you were thinking, "Yeah, right! This all sounds wonderful, but can principals really find the time and make the commitment to meet with each other and study their practice?" It is normal and natural for principals to like the idea of meeting with a collaborative group of colleagues regularly and believe in the process of learning communities and inquiry in the abstract but protest a lack of time in their daily lives. Roland Barth (2001) informs us that one reason it is so difficult for school leaders to become learners is lack of time, but he reminds us, "For principals, as for all of us, protesting a lack of time is another way of saying other things are more important and perhaps more comfortable" (p. 157). To address the constraints of time, districts may consider rethinking the traditional "principal meeting format." If principals are to become instructional leaders, then district leaders need to recognize the importance of collaboration and restructure their meetings to facilitate this type of interaction. Supervisors of principals send a powerful message to school-based leaders when they alter the format of the scheduled times principals come together to allow them time, on a regular basis, to collaborate and study their practice. When district leaders disseminate operational and organizational initiatives that are "information only" using e-mail or handouts, principals reduce the amount of time dedicated to "sit and get" and increase their opportunities to grow professionally in collaboration with their peers. Giving school-based leaders the gift of time for structured conversation and collegial support to investigate real-life dilemmas not only reinforces the notion that leaders must be learners but also sets the conditions so that principals see inquiry as part of their daily work.

> I realized that I consistently scheduled my school time to meet with teachers, parents, teacher union representatives, and community leaders; monitor cafeteria duty and bus duty; and visit classrooms. I was constantly focusing on helping others, but I allowed virtually no time in my day for me to grow as a leader. I came to understand that although I exercised much control over the events of a school day, I had no apparent control over my day. (R. Ovalle, principal, personal communication, 2010)

With this insight, Rob began blocking time in his calendar for his personal professional development. Reminding his secretary that this was a period of "do not disturb" and putting processes in place for others to handle day-to-day crises, he was able to experience the power of reflective practice. Scheduling time to meet with his PPLC became a priority. Surrounded by supportive colleagues, Rob was able to discuss troubling problems and to discover that he was not alone in his struggles. Together, his PPLC formulated questions; developed action steps; and identified, collected, and analyzed data to clarify their thinking. Finally, they celebrated what they had learned with others. As Rob reflected on his experience with the inquiry process, he realized the magic of a learning community dedicated to improving one's practice and the importance of taking time for oneself.

Although it appears straightforward that principals should schedule time to reflect, conduct research, and talk with other principals, school leaders are often drawn into immediate crises that take precedence over all else. School-based administrators are quick problem solvers, and this type of swift response is often the reason they are successful principals in the first place. In fact, many principals thrive on the challenge of moving quickly and decisively from one problem to another. For them, reflection, research, and conversation about dilemmas can often feel uncomfortable and drawn out, almost antithetical to the harried pace at which they are used to working. Hence, it is critical to provide ongoing reinforcement to school-based leaders who engage in the work of inquiry. Successful principal-inquirers need both the corroboration of a group of colleagues (the PPLC) as well as ongoing support from senior district administrators. This support must also include creating a safe place for principals to "wonder" about their practice. Senior district administrators must send a message to principals that they have both the autonomy and responsibility to make their schools better and that their individual and collective inquiry is both welcomed and expected.

Another challenge of establishing a PPLC can be a sort of competitiveness among principals. Although principals are delighted to share their successes, they rarely admit to uncertainty or lack of answers. Bringing principals together into learning communities where community agreements or norms are established and honored provides principals with the space to freely grapple with genuine dilemmas. Establishing a way of work for the PPLC and holding members accountable for their collaboration is a critical component of inquiry. Although individual PPLCs establish their own community agreements or norms, the list often includes the following:

- Speak and listen from the heart (the goal is understanding, not agreement);
- Monitor equity of participation;
- Acknowledge one another as equals;
- Assume goodwill;
- Trust the process;
- Be present (on time, cell phones muted, in the room); and
- Expect it to be messy at times.

Once established, these agreements need to be revisited frequently, usually at every meeting. Community agreements, like time, are a necessary structure for the important work of inquiry (see also the NSRF protocol "Forming Ground Rules" at http://nsrfharmony.org/protocol/doc/forming_ground_rules.pdf).

How Can You Make PPLCs Happen in Your District?

While it is clear that time, and protesting the lack of it, will be the biggest challenge to the establishment of PPLCs in a district, it can be done. One successful way many districts have met this challenge head on is by reconfiguring their district administrative team meeting. These meetings are often consumed by information giving. By taking stock of the ways time is utilized at these meetings, superintendents and other central-office staff often discover that much of the information that is being announced at these meetings can be communicated in other ways (e.g., e-mail), and PPLC work can take the place of the time "saved." Sometimes it is difficult for central office staff to shift the ways they utilize meeting time. Yet, rather than ask the question, "Can we really afford the time at our district administrative team meetings to do this?" ask the question, "Given the multiple benefits of PPLC work, can we, as a district, afford not to do this?" By safeguarding at least a portion of time during the districtwide administrative team meetings that already are a part of all principals' work and already are established in their calendars, PPLCs can beat the biggest factor that works against their establishment: lack of time.

What Role Does the Establishment of PPLCs Play in a Districtwide Professional Development Program?

There are two compelling reasons why a focus on administrators learning in community and studying their own administrative practice is an important piece of the puzzle to assemble a powerful, districtwide professional development program. First, the PPLC represents a microcosm of the districtwide professional development program, and it sets an example that can be replicated across a school district. A districtwide professional development program that embraces an inquiry stance communicates to the entire district that this is the way of work throughout the district. By examining the successes and struggles of a PPLC, district leaders can identify processes and structures necessary to ensure that all educators, with the support of other professionals, progress and continue to grow professionally throughout their careers.

Second, principals who have experienced the power of studying their practice in community and publicly celebrating their inquiry results understand and can predict the struggles, roadblocks, and unintended outcomes a teacher may encounter during inquiry. Because of their shared experience, the principals are well prepared to coach and support their staffs as they embark on a journey that establishes and sustains a school-wide inquiry stance.

WHERE CAN I LEARN MORE ABOUT PPLCs?

There are some great resources available to launch the PPLC work in your district.

- Dana, N. F. (2009). *Leading with passion and knowledge: The principal as action researcher*. Thousand Oaks, CA: Corwin. This book takes principals step-by-step through each component of the inquiry process, from finding your wondering to analyzing data and sharing your work with others. The text elaborates in great detail on many of the concepts introduced in this chapter. For example, one chapter is devoted to the nine passions that principals use to define a question for study. Many examples of principals' inquiries associated with each passion are shared.

- Militello, M., Rallis, S. F., & Goldring, E. B. (2009). *Leading with inquiry and action: How principals improve teaching and learning*. Thousand Oaks, CA: Corwin. This book presents a systematic process for data collection, decision making, and action steps to improve professional practice. It serves primarily as a guide for principals who wish to scaffold teachers in inquiry.

- Byrne-Jimenez, M., & Orr, M. T. (2007). *Developing effective principals through collaborative inquiry*. New York: Teachers College Press. This book thoroughly explores the relationship between collaboration and professional learning for principals. With chapters devoted to both collaboration and facilitation, the book is a guide for supporting novice and struggling principals as well as providing new learning opportunities for veterans.

- Joyce, B. R., & Showers, B. (2002). *Student achievement through staff development* (3rd ed.). Alexandria, VA: ASCD. This book focuses on the notion that student achievement is directly related to educators' systematic inquiry and learning. The primary emphasis is inquiry about curriculum and instruction that helps students reach high levels of academic achievement.

REVIEW AND LOOKING AHEAD

In this chapter, we

1. defined the principal professional learning community;

2. discussed the benefits and challenges of PPLC work;

3. suggested ways to make PPLCs happen in a district;

4. reviewed the role PPLCs play in the districtwide professional development program; and

5. suggested additional resources for learning more about principal inquiry and the power of principals learning in community.

In Chapter 2, we will illustrate the ways PPLC work can play out in a district over the course of an entire school year, using the story of Carol and Sylvia's work with their colleague Bob Poth and the ways they restructured administrative team meetings as PPLCs to engage 37 principals in the important work of inquiry.

2

The Principal Professional Learning Community in Practice

The Story of Carol, Sylvia, Bob, and 37 Principals

More innovative principal development models are needed, models that embrace a more constructivist approach and build on, rather than underestimate, the skills and knowledge that principals already posses.

—Monica Byrne-Jimenez and Margaret Terry Orr (2007, p. 9)

Carol had served in a variety of positions in Pinellas County Schools, from classroom teacher to assistant superintendent of curriculum and instruction. Although she enjoyed all of her 22 years working in the 26th-largest district in the nation, she was most excited about becoming a regional superintendent. In her new role, Carol would oversee 37 elementary schools, including curriculum, facilities, operations, and the direct supervision of building administrators.

One passion that Carol took with her into this new position was a commitment to change the way school leaders viewed professional development. Two years prior to Carol's beginning this new position, the district had begun to introduce teacher inquiry into the district professional development plan. Teachers who had engaged in the process described it as the best professional development they had ever experienced. Although the concept of teacher inquiry had caught fire in one pocket of the school district and was spreading rapidly, Carol knew that if administrators did not understand, support, and value the process of inquiry, the fire that had been ignited in her district would eventually burn out.

As she began to envision her work with the administrators of 37 different buildings, it was clear to Carol that if administrators were to be instructional leaders focused on supporting the learning of their teachers, they first needed to experience and feel for themselves the power of inquiry and learning in community.

Carol knew that she could use the monthly full-day administrative meetings to help principals experience powerful professional learning for themselves. Carol was determined to revitalize these traditional "sit and get" meetings at which principals gathered to discuss operational issues and hear about the latest instructional techniques, state mandates, and research-based strategies. Such meetings, although important and necessary, were packed with a month-long pile-up of information to share with the building-level administrators. They were not a model for effective professional learning. Traditionally, at these meetings principals learned new information or instructional strategies, which they were to take back to their school community and teach to their faculties. The experience was frequently described by principals as learning to swim one day and being required to swim the English Channel the next.

And so, Carol embarked on a year-long journey to revitalize the traditional monthly principal meetings to create a culture in which administrators could feel the power of learning in community and focus solely on their own learning without worrying about translating what they were learning to others. The goal was to create a space in which each principal could experience professional learning at its best through the process of inquiry, by retooling the traditional regional meeting to function as a principal professional learning community.

Carol was not working in isolation. Bob, a principal colleague, had been designated by the district as a "principal on special assignment" to work with Carol to oversee this region. In addition, Pinellas County Schools had developed a strong partnership with a university that provided a wonderful resource called a *professor in residence*: a university faculty member who lived in Pinellas County and worked with the district on various professional development initiatives. Having coached many teachers in the process of inquiry, Sylvia, the Pinellas County professor in residence, joined this inquiry journey. Carol, Bob, and Sylvia met regularly to plan and debrief the regional meetings over the course of the next year.

JUNE

Articulating Some Important Aspects of the Work With Principals

Carol, Bob, and Sylvia's June planning meetings laid the foundation for the year. To begin, they focused on the important distinction between congeniality and collegiality, a concept that Roland Barth had written about extensively. Administrators were extremely comfortable with, and good at, congenial relationships. Congenial relationships are friendly, pleasant interactions like discussing the status of the basketball team, vacation plans, and retirements or holiday events. Although congeniality is a necessary element of a positive learning environment, a culture of congeniality alone would not encourage principal learning or the construction of new knowledge or growth of the inquiry process. For principals to learn together, they must also develop collegial relationships in which they can talk about difficult issues and share their practice with one another. The planners knew that in order for regional meetings to be transformed, they would need to balance preserving a culture of congeniality while nudging the administrators into collegial relationships.

The planning threesome agreed that to change the thinking and actions of administrators, specific conditions, structures, and processes needed to be established that would foster collegiality (principals thinking and learning with and from each other). These conditions, structures, and processes included concrete, structured conversations about the work of an administrator; thoughtful reflection; opportunities to observe each other at work and talk about the observations; personal individualized growth plans; and opportunities to teach each other about what they were learning.

As trained National School Reform Faculty facilitators, Carol, Bob, and Sylvia had developed tools they could draw upon to create the conditions, structures, and processes necessary for the work ahead. One of the most valuable tools they would utilize in their work with principals was the NSRF protocols: a series of timed, structured steps the conversation among a group of principals would follow during regional meetings. In order to create the time at each regional meeting for collegial conversation structured by protocols, operational issues and informational items would be communicated in writing (via e-mail) rather than verbally.

Another planning aspect of their work focused on understanding and honoring the mental makeup of administrators. Carol, Bob, and Sylvia knew that once they left regional meetings, principals would be faced with a multitude of responsibilities when they returned to school. Unless they helped principals see the ways the regional meetings could help them with their "regular everyday work," the experiences of the regional meeting could easily be forgotten and shelved until the next monthly meeting. With this in mind, they decided each regional meeting would conclude

> . . . it would be crucial to listen to the voices of the principals . . .

with a gentle discussion of how the experiences of the meeting could be translated into something they could do back at their school; this would enable principals to use the knowledge and skills they were learning to make a difference in the work they were doing every day.

The planners knew that creating a culture in which principals worked as a community of learners would take patience and it would be crucial to listen to the voices of the principals as fresh ways of working and learning together were introduced.

They also knew that without a clearly defined plan, they could easily get derailed by "urgent operational issues," state mandates, or even push back and resistance from the school leaders themselves. To address these concerns, they decided to establish a principals' advisory group. This group would meet with Carol, Bob, and Sylvia regularly to help them take the "pulse" of the learning that was occurring during regional meetings.

Carol resisted the urge to place only those principals who would champion the new way of work in the advisory group. Instead, she gathered a diverse collection of principals that included master principals, new principals, principals who were quick to embrace innovation, and principals who were more traditional. She knew it would be just as important to listen to the principals who might be hesitant to work differently as it would be to listen to the principals who would be excited about and embrace the new ways they were working during regional meetings. At the close of their last planning session, Carol, Sylvia, and Bob committed to listening to the voices of the advisory board as a guide for their work. The principal's advisory board would provide valuable insights and become a critical factor in the success of the PPLC.

JULY

Getting Started on the Right Foot

As the planners developed the framework for the first regional meeting of the year, they knew the principals would ask, "*Why* are we doing this?" Therefore, it would be important to help their principals develop the big picture reason for restructuring their regional meetings to function as an inquiry-oriented PPLC. It would be important to establish the "why" before they even began talking specifically about inquiry as a tool for prin-

> It would be important to establish the "why."

cipal professional development. They selected Mike Schmoker's (2004) *Phi Delta Kappan* article, "Tipping Point:

From Feckless Reform to Substantive Instructional Improvement" for the principals to read and discuss.

Although this article would provide content for the principals to frame their inquiry work, Carol and her colleagues also knew they needed to focus on the process of working together because most principals were not only unaccustomed to talking with each other, they certainly weren't used to opening up, reflecting, and taking time to consider the many different perspectives of their practice. As a companion to the Schmoker article, Carol selected "Willing to Be Disturbed" by Margaret Wheatley (2002), which discusses the importance of being open to and curious about new ideas and ways of thinking that may be different from your own. Together these articles would encourage the principals to open up to new possibilities.

Since these principals had not been used to sharing and discussing their practice with one another, Carol, Sylvia, and Bob planned a relatively low-risk small group activity so the principals could get a feel for what it would be like to talk with one another in a systematic way. Hence, they selected one of the National School Reform Faculty's text-based protocols, "The Four A's" (http://nsrfharmony.org/protocol/doc/4_a_text.pdf), to structure the discussion about the two readings and to enable the principals to experience how learning community work might feel.

At the July regional meeting, Carol took a deep breath and began to explain the activity: "OK, everyone, now we are going to do something a little different at this meeting than you are used to doing at regional meetings. Each month that we meet, I want to devote a little bit of our time together to our learning as principals. Roland Barth talks about principals not taking care of their own professional development, and that taking care of ourselves as administrators is a prerequisite to our ability to take care of the teachers and students in our charge."

To help illustrate the importance of taking care of oneself first, Carol used the oxygen mask metaphor and reminded the principals that on an airplane, you are instructed to first secure the oxygen mask on your own face, so you can then help others. Carol concluded this metaphor by saying, "So, we're going to spend a portion of our meetings each month securing our own oxygen masks, so that we are better able to help others. To help set the tone for the ways we are going to use some of our regional meeting time, today we are going to read and discuss two articles, 'Tipping Point: From Feckless Reform to Substantive Instructional Improvement,' and 'Willing to Be Disturbed.'"

The Four A's Protocol

Carol handed out both articles, and as the principals read the first article, they highlighted and wrote notes in the margin to answer the following four questions:

- What **assumptions** does the author of the text hold?
- What do you **agree** with in the text?

- What do you want to **argue** with in the text?
- What parts of the text do you want to **aspire** to?

In small groups, the principals began a series of rounds talking about the article in light of each of the "A's," beginning with assumptions and then taking the other three "A's" one at a time. Each member of the group had one minute to share about each of the four "A's" in turn. This allowed the principals to respond to the article in a small group setting and ensured that every principal would participate in the discussion and no one principal would dominate. As the discussion unfolded, principals had the opportunity to honestly *hear* and understand their colleagues' perspectives. This was a critical first step to professional learning and collaboration.

The activity concluded with a general discussion focused on the question, "What does this mean for our work as principals?" The principals debriefed the activity by identifying how they might improve their discussions in the future as well as what their next steps would be toward focusing on their own professional development as principals for the coming school year. The same protocol was repeated with the second article, giving the principals a second exposure to a structured discussion in which listening and individual perspectives were valued. Again, the learning experience concluded with the group having a few minutes to talk about "how it felt" to work together with structure and clear direction.

Ending the learning experiences, Carol asked the principals to consider how they might use what they learned from the articles as well as how they might use the four "A's" protocol back at their own school. Spontaneously, several principals volunteered that they planned to read both articles and use the four "A's" process with their administrative teams.

August

Growing a Community of Learners

As Carol reviewed the first meeting with Bob and Sylvia, Bob kiddingly remarked, "I'm not sure how many you converted, but at least no one booed you." Although Bob's intent was merely to add some levity to the intensity of this work, his statement worried Carol. Were the principals just going through the motions because Carol was the regional superintendent, and they felt they needed to comply? Did this need to comply with authority and to seemingly please Carol inhibit their honest responses to the two articles they had read and debriefed together? Did these principals feel comfortable discussing their thinking openly and honestly not only with Carol, but with one another in a collegial fashion? To move from compliance and congenial learning to authentic,

> " . . . at least no one booed you."

collegial engagement, the planners realized that a safe environment where all learners' needs were honored was critical. In the excitement of focusing on revamping the way administrators worked together, the importance of establishing a shared set of guidelines that would help everyone participate in a respectful manner and encourage both feedback and action had been overlooked.

For the next regional meeting, the team decided that Bob would use the "Ground Rules" protocol to address this oversight (http://nsrfharmony .org/protocol/doc/forming_ground_rules.pdf). This protocol is designed to help people establish community agreements, and it provided an opportunity for Carol to be a participant in the learning community. The planners thought this would send a subtle message to the group, positioning Carol less as their regional superintendent and more as a colleague passionate about helping everyone learn and grow in their practice.

The planning group decided that once community agreements were established, the second regional meeting would also be the place to focus the principals' gaze on inquiry. Inquiry was not a new topic for the principals. In fact, action research was cited as an expectation for professional development by the state of Florida's Department of Education, and the principals were well aware that an increasing number of teachers were engaging in inquiry as a mechanism for teacher professional development in their district. What would be new for the principals would be the concept of applying the process of inquiry to their own work as administrators and actually taking some time to discuss the concept of inquiry and what it means—and doesn't mean—together.

Because inquiry had never been discussed with administrators in any in-depth way, the planning threesome knew each principal would have varying levels of experience and knowledge about the process. However, they avoided the temptation to do a traditional PowerPoint presentation to review the concept of inquiry in order to get everyone on the same page. Carol wanted the principals to continue to experience active learning rather than fall back into an old meeting structure of passively listening to reports and administrative directives. Rather than use PowerPoint, Carol wished to structure a discussion that would honor the principals' prior experiences with inquiry, give them an opportunity to chat about their conceptions of the inquiry process and the ways they are seeing it unfold in the district with teachers, generate questions they had about the process, and allow them to see the potential that engagement in the process of inquiry might hold for their professional development as principals. The planning team elected to use a diagram of the inquiry process to initiate conversation with the principals; they used the "Making Meaning" protocol (http://nsrfharmony.org/protocol/doc/making_meaning.pdf) to structure the conversation.

Setting the Ground Rules

As the principals gathered for the August meeting, Bob asked each principal to write on an index card what he or she would need from the others in order to do his or her very best work during the regional meetings. As an example, Bob shared that for him, "starting the meetings on time" was important, to honor the busy lives administrators have. After five minutes of silent writing, the principals had generated numerous ideas. The index cards were then grouped by similar statements and posted around the room on charts. Each principal received six "sticky dots" (the kind many people use to price items at garage sales) to use as they "read the room." Principals were instructed to walk around the room, read the index cards, think about what they noticed, and place their dots next to the statements that were most necessary for the best possible work to occur when they were together. Some principals put all six dots by one statement, while others used a single dot for each of six different conditions. Quickly, a visible consensus about the most important conditions for this group of learners was revealed. By allowing the group to first individually identify, then collectively merge their thoughts with very little risk for any principal, the administrators were able to discover what was critical to the success of the learning. The following statements received the most sticky dots, and the principals unanimously agreed that these "norms" would guide their work together at regional meetings during the year:

- Speak honestly; don't hold back.
- If you're going to say it in the parking lot, say it here.
- Be present (come on time, turn off cell phones/BlackBerries).
- Don't act like you understand when you don't.
- Assume goodwill; help each other.
- Trust each other and trust in the process of the work we are going to do together.
- Expect to be confused at times and not understand; that's OK.
- Embrace mistakes.

These established community agreements would be frequently revisited as collegial relationships grew stronger. It became a ritual to review community agreements at the start of each regional meeting.

Moving Into Inquiry

When Bob was finished facilitating the "Ground Rules" protocol, Carol shifted the focus of the meeting to inquiry by thanking Bob for his facilitation skills, acknowledging the importance of ground rules and community agreements, and opening a conversation about a powerful form of professional learning for teachers: inquiry. Carol acknowledged that the principals had different backgrounds and experiences with inquiry, sometimes referred to as action research, and she kicked off a discussion of the topic by handing out the Cycle of Inquiry Diagram adapted from the Southern Maine Partnership, one of the many models of inquiry available (see Figure 2.1).

Figure 2.1 Cycle of Inquiry

Adapted from *Cycle of Inquiry* developed by Southern Maine Partnership

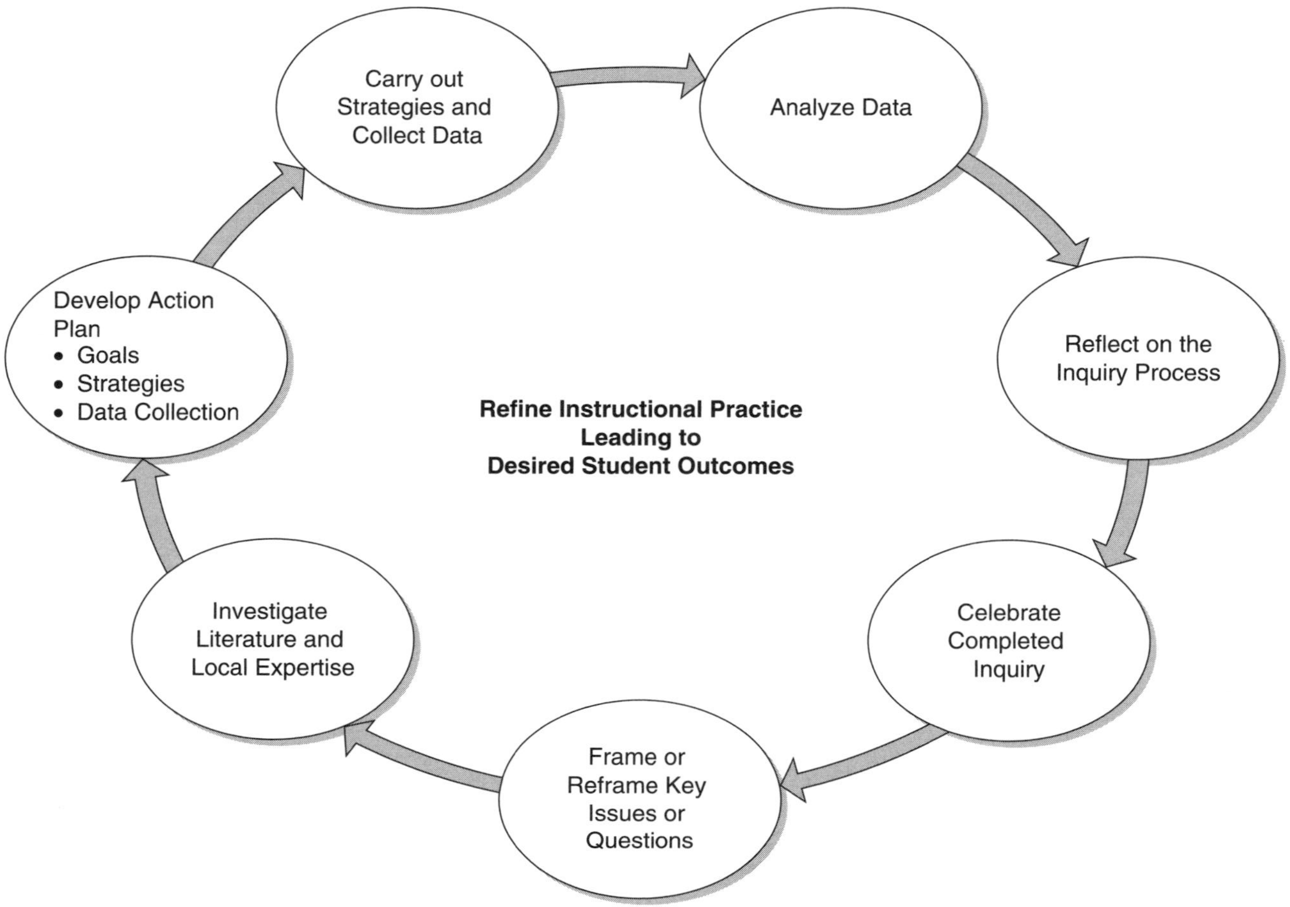

The inquiry process to the left is displayed as a cyclical process. In actual implementation, schools and individual teachers can enter the cycle at any point, and often move back and forth between steps. Desired Refined Instructional Practice and Student Outcomes are integral parts of the cycle of inquiry even though they are not displayed as a stage of the cycle. Refinement of these elements may happen at any stage of the cycle. In fact, these ideas should be revisited on a periodic basis in order to refine these elements.

Reflect on the Inquiry Process

Celebrate Completed Inquiry

Analyze Data

Frame or Reframe Key Issues or Questions

Refine Instructional Practice Leading to Desired Student Outcomes

Carry out Strategies and Collect Data

Investigate Literature and Local Expertise

Develop Action Plan
• Goals
• Strategies
• Data Collection

The principals took a few moments to look at this diagram in silence and then make some brief notes about aspects of it that they particularly noticed. Principals were reorganized in smaller groups of seven or eight to discuss the diagram using the "Making Meaning" protocol.

The Making Meaning Protocol

Each principal had the steps of the "Making Meaning" protocol in front of him or her on a handout while Carol explained that the principals had already completed the Step 1: Getting Started. In this step, everyone simply reads the text (or the diagram) and makes some notes.

In Step 2: Describing the Text, the principals answered the question, "What do we see?" In this step they focused on observations, not judgments. Step 3: Asking Questions About the Text required the groups to make a list of all the questions that came up for every member of the group. Questions could be general or specific. In Step 4: Speculation, the principals discussed the question, "What is significant about this diagram?" As the principals talked, insights, problems, or issues that they had about the diagram emerged. In Step 5: Implications, the participants deliberated about how the diagram might influence their work as principals. In the final step, Step 6: Reflections, administrators shared their reactions to using the protocol.

The principals were given five minutes for each of the steps and reminded to make notes as they discussed each step in their group. Finally, the entire group discussed the observations, questions, speculations, and implications generated in their small groups and reflected on the process of using this protocol to guide discussions.

> ". . . inquiry shouldn't be just for teachers."

The discussion helped the principals unearth their beliefs, experiences, conceptions, and misconceptions about the inquiry process. As the principals discussed their group responses to Step 5: Implications, one group shared, "It seemed to our group from the discussion of this diagram that inquiry shouldn't be just for teachers. As school leaders, shouldn't we be working to improve our own practice?"

By using the "Making Meaning" protocol, the principals had begun to realize that they were in charge of their own learning and that the inquiry process could be a powerful way to frame that learning. The principals agreed to use future meetings to help each other engage in the inquiry process as administrators.

The learning community work concluded with principals reflecting on the experiences they had with both the "Ground Rules" and "Making Meaning" protocols and how they could be helpful for the work they did at their schools. Principals saw the importance of using the community agreement process with an entire staff. One principal leaned forward in his chair, uncrossed his arms, and offered, "I'm ready to try inquiry. I'm going to talk about it with my administrative team."

SEPTEMBER AND OCTOBER

Common Dilemmas, Emerging Wonderings

During the next planning meeting, Carol, Bob, and Sylvia focused on helping the principals begin the inquiry process by developing wonderings and creating a plan for their own research at the next regional meetings.

Knowing good inquiry questions emerge from real-world dilemmas that principals face every day, the planning team agreed to devote time to helping principals name and discuss some dilemmas they face as administrators. Even broad dilemmas such as "too many state mandates," "too many struggling students," "not enough resources," or "no time to visit classes" had great potential for possible inquiry projects. For the September regional meeting, learning experiences were designed to help principals uncover genuine professional dilemmas that would eventually serve as the foundation for inquiry projects. The planning team anticipated the principals would likely share some common dilemmas and might elect to work in collaborative groups on their first administrative inquiries, so they were ready to encourage group work.

Once principals were arranged in smaller groups with a shared question articulated, they would need to develop a plan for data collection to gain insights into their questions. The planning team believed that having time to develop an inquiry brief would be a good experience for the principals. An *inquiry brief* is a one- or two-page action plan that lists five elements of the inquiry work: (1) a short background description of the dilemma that led to the question or wondering, (2) a statement of the wondering, (3) strategies the inquirer would use to collect data, (4) a plan to analyze the data, and (5) a month-by-month calendar of how the inquiry work would unfold over time.

At the September meeting, Carol asked the principals to sit in groups of eight, selecting learning partners with whom they felt they would be most comfortable sharing problems that they struggled with on a daily basis. These smaller working teams of principals became known as *critical friends groups* (CFGs), a term Carol, Sylvia, and Bob borrowed from the National School Reform Faculty. These smaller

> "If I'm in need of critical care, these are the folks who I want to save me."

clusters were called critical friends groups not because the principals were to be critical of each other, but as one principal so aptly phrased it, "If I'm in need of critical care, these are the folks who I want to save me." At this September meeting, the principals also discussed that the word *critical* in the phrase critical friends group meant that the people in their group were "a critical ingredient to further one another's learning." With these two statements, critical friends groups became another positive working condition for the principals. These CFGs eventually functioned not just during the regional meeting, but, once the principals began their inquiries, they met voluntarily after work and even on weekends.

In their newly formed CFGs, the principals developed a list of dilemmas: school problems that keep them awake at night or issues that got in the way of doing what is important for the success of the school. The principals focused only on identifying dilemmas and specifically refrained from identifying solutions to these problems.

As the lists of dilemmas evolved, the principals posted them around the room. It was easy to notice that the principals shared many common problems. Carol, Sylvia, and Bob circulated from group to group, helping each CFG frame its dilemmas as potential inquiry questions.

When the time came for the October meeting, the principals immediately got into their CFGs to work further on their inquiries by tackling the next step: developing an inquiry brief. This would include each group committing to one question they wished to explore together, naming the data collection strategies they would employ, making a plan for data analysis, and creating a timeline for the implementation of their inquiries. However, Carol, Bob, and Sylvia noticed that at this meeting, the principals were spending more time asking questions and looking puzzled than they were engaging in thoughtful, meaningful conversation. The planning team noticed all was not well and that they would need to regroup in order to move forward.

NOVEMBER

Slowing Down to Speed Up

After the somewhat confusing ending to the October meeting, Carol, Sylvia, and Bob revisited the community agreements they had established only months ago. Two of the agreement statements, "Trust the process of the work we are going to do together" and "Expect to be confused at times and not understand," seemed to resonate loudly as they prepared for the next principal meeting. Based upon input from the principals' advisory group, there was general consensus that many of the principals were confused about the purpose and steps of inquiry. Although most had identified a wondering, the principals needed additional support and guidance to develop powerful inquiry projects. The planning team determined that because administrators had different levels of prior knowledge of and experience with inquiry, time should be built into the monthly meetings for principals to clarify and confirm their thinking and to learn more about the process itself. The team decided to use an elementary school strategy to assess the situation at the November meeting: The KWL chart.

The KWL Protocol

As principals gathered in their CFGs for the November meeting, Carol explained the KWL activity, and each CFG made a three-column chart, with the columns labeled K, W, and L, respectively.

In the K column the principals wrote what they *knew* about inquiry when they started in July. In the W column the principals charted what they still *wanted* to learn about inquiry, and in the L column they listed what they had *learned* about inquiry since the PPLC work was initiated in July. As the KWL charts grew, principals who were more experienced with the inquiry process took on the role of helping others clarify their understanding of certain elements of inquiry. Important themes emerged that would be utilized to frame the work for the next regional meetings, including the principals' need for more information on how the process of inquiry differed from traditional forms of educational research, how to collect and analyze data in ways other than just looking at test scores, and how to fit the process of inquiry into what they do as a normal and natural part of their work day.

As had become the tradition for ending their PPLC time together, the group discussed what they might be able to take back and use at their school. Many remarked that although they had seen a KWL chart used in the classroom, they had not considered its use for adult learning. They noted that the KWL strategy could be used to gather information from their staff on numerous topics they were currently addressing, from RTI implementation, to school discipline, and even teachers' understanding of the union contract. Finally, the principals expressed their appreciation to Carol, Bob, and Sylvia for slowing down the learning and creating an opportunity for the principals to voice their feelings about inquiry in a productive way.

DECEMBER THROUGH MARCH

Supporting the Process

Over the next four months, the principals revisited the KWL chart and adapted it as their knowledge grew through readings and activities they did together to understand the inquiry process as they were living it that school year. Two resources that were helpful to the principals in developing a better understanding of critical aspects of the inquiry process were the books *Leading With Passion and Knowledge: The Principal as Action Researcher* (Dana, 2009) and *Leading With Inquiry and Action: How Principals Improve Teaching and Learning* (Militello, Rallis, & Goldring, 2009).

There were two recurring questions in the "Want to Know" column of one group's KWL chart:

- Is it important to set up control groups when we design our inquiries?
- Do we have to do a big, hairy, literature review like I did for my dissertation work?

These questions confirmed that principals needed to understand the differences between traditional educational research and principal inquiry. Reading a short excerpt from the book *Living the Questions: A Guide for Teacher Researchers* (Hubbard & Power, 1999) called "Little r and Big R" clarified the principals' misconceptions.

Little r and Big R

When we first talk with teachers about the possibilities for research in their professional lives, they often recount negative experiences with research and stereotypical views of what researchers do. As teacher Julie Ford explains,

> When I think of research, I think of the Big R type and long hours in the library, notes that could fill a novel, and a bibliography several pages long. I think of tension and stress lurking in the shadows. Feeling as I do about Research, the thought of conducting it in my classroom didn't curl my toes. But as I read classroom-based research, I felt as though a door was beginning to open. My definition of research took a turn, and that familiar twinge of anxiety didn't come rushing forward.

Teachers are surprised and delighted to realize that research can focus on problems they are trying to solve in their own classrooms. At its best, teacher research is a natural extension of good teaching. Observing students closely, analyzing their needs, and adjusting the curriculum to fit the needs of all students have always been important skills demonstrated by fine teachers.

Teacher research involves collecting and analyzing data as well as presenting it to others in a systematic way. But this research process involves the kinds of skills and classroom activities that already are a part of the classroom environment. As Glenda Bissex writes, a teacher-researcher is not a split personality, but a more complete teacher. While research is labor-intensive, so is good teaching. And the labor is similar for teachers, because the end goal is the same—to create the best possible learning environment for students.

[The research agenda] of most teachers are a kind of "dance" between teachers, students, and learning. Teacher-researchers rarely seek to initiate and carry out studies that have large-scale implications for education policy. Unlike large-scale education research, teacher research has a primary purpose of helping the teacher-researcher understand her students and improve her practice in specific, concrete ways. Teacher research studies can and do lead to large-scale education change. But for most teacher-researchers, the significance of the study is in how it informs and changes her own teaching.

Lawrence Stenhouse noted that the difference between the teacher-researcher and the large-scale education researcher is like the difference between a farmer with a huge agricultural business to maintain and the "careful gardener" tending a backyard plot:

In agriculture the equation of invested input against gross yield is all: it does not matter if individual plants fail to thrive or die so long as the cost of saving them is greater than the cost of losing them. . . . This does not apply to the careful gardener whose labour is not costed, but a labour of love. He wants each of his plants to thrive, and he can treat each one individually. Indeed he can grow a hundred different plants in his garden and differentiate his treatment of each, pruning his roses, but not his sweet peas. Gardening rather than agriculture is the analogy for education. (Rudduck and Hopkins, 1985, 26)

This view of the teacher-researcher as a "careful gardener" is the image we hold in our minds of the ideal teacher-researcher—not a scientist in a lab coat, staring down at a "research subject" (a kid!), but a human being in the midst of teaching, carefully weighing the value of different ways of teaching and learning (pp. 3–4).

The Text Rendering Protocol

As had become standard practice for all PPLC discussions at the regional meetings, Carol, Sylvia, and Bob scaffolded the principals' discussion of this piece of text using a protocol called "Text Rendering" (http://nsrfharmony.org/protocol/doc/text_rendering.pdf). In this protocol, the principals read the text and underlined one sentence, one phrase, and one single word that they believed to be particularly important to the inquiry work they were doing as administrators. Next, in round-robin fashion, each principal shared his or her sentence, phrase, and one word with his or her CFG. As had happened numerous times when utilizing a protocol, animated conversation regarding why they had chosen specific sentences, phrases, or words emerged naturally, and the CFGs concluded their conversation focusing on new insights they now had about traditional educational research versus the type of research they were engaging in as principals. By engaging in this text rendering exercise, the principals were inspired to think of the research they were doing in a much more natural- istic and meaningful way.

In addition to engaging in some whole group discussion and activity about critical aspects of the inquiry process at each regional meeting from November through March, principals worked in their smaller CFGs, talk- ing through and working on their individual inquiries. For example, one group of eight principals wanted to improve the feedback they provided to their teachers, particularly in relation to their implementation of the classroom walk-through process. In September, this group of principals expressed a shared frustration that although they were going through all the motions of the classroom walk-through, it appeared that neither they nor their teachers found meaning in the process. Together, the principals crafted one collective wondering that guided their inquiry: In what ways will focusing our classroom walk throughs on teacher-selected growth areas improve the process for us as administrators as well as for our teach- ers? During CFG time at the November meeting, this group read excerpts from *The Three Minute Classroom Walk-Through: Changing School Supervisory Practice One Teacher at a Time* (Downey, Steffy, English, Frase, & Poston, 2004) and debriefed the reading using a text-based protocol. At the December meeting, the group worked together to devise a plan they would all implement at their schools to improve the walk-through process after the holiday break. At subsequent meetings, members of the group took turns sharing data they had collected when trying out this new plan at their school. Using a protocol to guide their analysis of the data, the group members marveled at the ways their newly implemented procedure was playing out in their individual administrative practice, and they real- ized that by looking at their data collectively as well as reading and sharing additional literature related to classroom walk throughs, they continually refined and improved their supervisory practice.

APRIL AND MAY

Sharing and Celebrating

Fortunately, Pinellas County Schools already had a yearly Inquiry Celebra- tion in place at which teachers from across the district presented their inquiries. To date, this celebration had included teacher presentations only. Although administrators had attended this event in the past, none had ever presented an inquiry of his or her own. Principals thought about how they could discuss their inquiry with others at the April meeting and worked together to plan their presentations. At the May celebration, the principals' sessions were well attended. The principals were proud to share their professional learning and answer questions about the inquiry process from their fellow administrators. After the Pinellas Inquiry Celebration was over, small groups of administrators continued to come together to share their projects with each other; many of the principal CFGs continued to meet on their own time to discuss plans for next year; and the principal inquirers spoke in glowing terms about their first experiences with inquiry.

The school year was coming to an end. Graduations, end of the year parties, report cards, hiring new teachers, honoring retiring teachers, class lists, and book orders had the attention of these 37 school administrators. Yet, despite the hectic pressure of bringing closure to another school year, these administrators knew they had experienced something special: the beginning of a transformation of professional development. They were ready to take this process into their schools and committed to taking inquiry to their teachers and coaching them in the process of inquiry-oriented PLC work.

QUESTIONS FOR DISCUSSION

Part I: For the Administrator

Part I of this text focused on the principal's role in building a successful districtwide professional development plan. Reflect on Part I and apply what you've learned from the two chapters to your own context by answering the following questions:

1. Carol benefitted greatly from collaboration with her colleagues, Sylvia and Bob, as she facilitated and led the PPLC work. In your own district, who might work together as you plan and assess learning community activities for administrators?

2. Carol, Sylvia, and Bob utilized a number of different protocols to structure the dialogue that occurred with their PPLCs over the course of the school year (i.e., The Four A's, Ground Rules, Making Meaning From Text, KWL, Text Rendering).

   • Which one of these protocols would you feel most comfortable using yourself and why?
   • How and when could you use this protocol in your own practice?
   • Which of these protocols would you feel least comfortable using yourself and why?
   • When and why might you use this protocol, and what, if anything, might help you become more comfortable with its use?

3. Carol, Sylvia, and Bob experienced a tumultuous time as their PPLC work with administrators unfolded over the school year, when principals felt confused about their inquiry work and began to grumble about their new way of working with one another.

   • What actions did Carol, Sylvia, and Bob take to address the "unrest" that was beginning to develop?
   • What helped Carol, Sylvia, and Bob turn the situation around and get the work back on track?

4. What do you feel would be the greatest benefit to establishing PPLCs across your district?

5. What do you feel would be the greatest challenge to establishing PPLCs across your district? How might this challenge be addressed?

PART II

The Teacher's Role

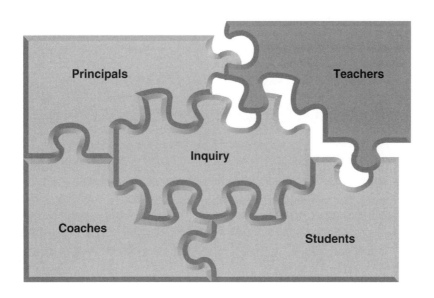

3

The Inquiry-Oriented PLC

The most enjoyable aspect of my work as a principal this year was observing teachers explore their passions and implement innovative practices through the inquiry process. In this day and age when many teachers complain that their flexibility and creativity is stifled due to standardized testing and curriculum, allowing teachers the opportunity to implement and study a passion empowers them to continuously explore ways to improve their effectiveness and grow in their craft.

—Michael Moss, Principal, Fuguitt Elementary School

There are few conversations about teaching these days that don't include talk about teacher quality. Yet, the dialogue is often political, consumed with controversial solutions for improving teacher quality such as linking teacher pay to student performance. Absent from the pervasive political conversations about improving teacher *quality* across the country is dialogue that focuses on what it would take to improve teacher *learning*. Clearly, there is a direct relationship between improving the quality of a teacher's work in the classroom and the teacher's capacity to learn, change, and grow in his or her instructional practices. This capacity is dependent upon a teacher's ability to identify critical issues, problems, tensions, or dilemmas that are impacting or inhibiting student learning in the classroom; design an informed plan of action to address the identified issue; and continually assess the relationship between the implementation of the instructional action and student learning. Teacher quality is unleashed when teachers' basic work is "renormed around identifying, striving to solve, and continually revisiting critical problems" (Copland, 2003, p. 376).

One simple word that captures this process by which teachers can improve their professional practice is *inquiry*. Deana Ferguson, a teacher in Pinellas County, describes eloquently what happens to a teacher who participates in inquiry:

> I realized that I had been trying to figure out something for reading comprehension for years . . . I began to research the use of graphic organizers using the steps of inquiry, which helped me to stay on track . . . it was not extra work; it probably saved me some time since I had the inquiry process to follow. It was my first stepping stone into what I hope is a long, inquiry-filled career.

Roland Barth (1990) likens the transformative impact of inquiry on teachers to the art of the potter:

> Just as potters cannot teach others to craft in clay without setting their own hands to work at the wheel, so teachers cannot fully teach others the excitement, the difficulty, the patience, and the satisfaction that accompany learning without themselves engaging in the messy, frustrating, and reworking "clay" of learning. Inquiry for teachers can take place both in and out of the view of students, but to teacher and student alike there must be continuous evidence that it is occurring. For when teachers observe, examine, question, and reflect on their ideas and develop new practices that lead toward their ideals, students are alive. When teachers stop growing, so do their students. (p. 50)

Once again, building on the work of Roland Barth, this chapter introduces the inquiry-oriented learning community as an effective structure to support teachers in their professional growth, thereby enhancing teacher quality and student achievement throughout a school district.

WHAT IS AN INQUIRY-ORIENTED LEARNING COMMUNITY?

Combining the best of what we know about action research and professional learning communities, an *inquiry-oriented PLC* is defined as a group of teaching professionals (approximately 6–12 colleagues) who meet regularly to learn from practice through structured dialogue and engage in continuous cycles of inquiry (articulating a wondering, collecting data to gain insights into the wondering, analyzing data, making improvements in practice based on what was learned, and sharing learning with others). Inquiry-oriented learning communities create the time and space, in a school or across schools, for teachers to come together to observe, examine, question, and reflect on student work and student learning in their classrooms and schools. By using this process, teachers are engaged in continuous learning about practice that is intimately intertwined with the learning their students are doing in their own classrooms.

Similar to the PPLC from Chapter 1, there are different ways an inquiry-oriented learning community can function: shared inquiry, parallel inquiry, and intersecting inquiry (see Figure 3.1).

Figure 3.1   Three Types of Inquiry-Oriented PLCs

Three Types of Inquiry-Oriented PLCs	
Inquiry-Oriented PLC: A group of teaching professionals (approximately 6 to 12 colleagues) who meet regularly to learn from practice through structured dialogue and engage in continuous cycles of inquiry (articulating a wondering, collecting data to gain insights into the wondering, analyzing data, making improvements in practice based on what was learned, and sharing learning with others).	
1. Shared Inquiry	Learning community members define and conduct a single inquiry together.
2. Parallel Inquiry	Learning community members conduct individual, independent inquiry projects but work collectively in their learning community to support each other's individual endeavor.
3. Intersecting Inquiry	Learning community members engage in individual inquiry projects that focus on the same topic, but they explore different questions or wonderings about that topic.

In *shared inquiry,* the teachers in the PLC define and conduct a single inquiry together.

One learning community we observed conducted a shared inquiry around the questions, "How do we create more culturally responsive teaching in our classrooms? and "What happens to student learning when we create more culturally responsive teaching?" All the teachers in this PLC committed to collecting and analyzing a variety of data to gain insights into their questions. For example, at the beginning of their work together the group members decided to distribute a survey to parents and students, to better understand their own goals as well as expectations they had of the school. During most of the year, the group saved student work samples, tracked student growth on assessments, and kept notes from peer observations to help them make sense of their ability to transfer new ideas about culturally responsive teaching to the classroom. Each of the members also committed to keeping a journal that included field notes as well as personal reflections on his or her teaching. Finally, they decided that by asking students to complete feedback sheets after engaging in culturally relevant teaching, they would be including student voices in the findings of their inquiry. All these data were discussed, analyzed, and debated at their PLC meetings at various times over the course of the school year.

An imperative component of any teacher inquiry is that it must evoke passion from the teacher-inquirer. Thus, a prerequisite for a learning community to engage in a shared inquiry is a shared passion for the same topic. This often happens naturally when a learning community's goals are aligned with a school improvement plan, emerge from analyzing the results of student performance on standardized tests, or result from a desire to figure out the implications for the adoption of a new curriculum or a new state or federal mandate. However, a shared passion for a single topic among all members of a learning community does not always emerge because teachers are unique individuals who have different interests, have different levels of experience, and have strengths in different components of teaching. If teachers in the same learning community have different questions about practice, then they may choose to engage in parallel inquiry.

Parallel inquiry occurs when members of a learning community conduct individual inquiry projects but work collectively in their learning community to support each other's individual endeavors. Parallel inquiry comes from the "parallel play" concept discussed in the early childhood literature. In parallel play, toddlers may sit in a sandbox, just inches apart from each other, and be enthralled with their individual exploration of the sand. They are each immersed in their own activity within the same physical space. Likewise, when teachers engage in parallel inquiry, their "playmates" are teaching colleagues in the same learning community, their "sand" is the complexities that are arising from their own classrooms, and their "sandbox" is their school. Unlike parallel play, however, in which the two toddlers are often oblivious of each other and rarely interact as they play, when engaging in parallel inquiry, teachers support each other's individual endeavors by helping to define a clear and coherent inquiry question, observing and collecting data for each other, and discussing data analysis and findings at PLC meetings.

In parallel inquiry, learning community members are engaging in inquiry to study and understand different topics, and the learning community meetings focus on supporting each individual in each component of the inquiry process. Sometimes teachers in a learning community engage in individual inquiry projects that focus on the same topic but explore different questions and wonderings about that topic. In this scenario, often the PLC's work is guided by one overarching general question, such as "What is the relationship between implementing different teaching strategies and our students' development as readers?" In one learning community, teachers explored the following subquestions related to this overarching topic:

- What is the relationship between the reading of fractured fairy tale plays and my students' fluency development?
- How do my struggling readers experience the use of the Interwrite Pad during reading instruction?
- What role do literature circles play in helping my advanced readers become more critical thinkers?
- How can I make my word wall in the literacy center more meaningful for my students?

When a learning community functions in this way, we say they are engaging in *intersecting inquiry.*

Regardless of the ways an inquiry-oriented professional learning community functions (engaging in shared inquiry, parallel inquiry, or intersecting inquiry), the most critical component is defining a powerful question to explore. Wonderings can take many different forms and relate to all subject areas (reading, writing, social sciences, mathematics, science, art and music, technology) and types of learners (English Language Learners; social, emotional, and behavioral supports). Figure 3.2 provides 40 examples of teacher wonderings.

Figure 3.2   40 Examples of Teacher Wonderings by Subject Area/Type of Learner

Subject Area/Type of Learner	Sample Inquiry Questions/Wonderings
Reading	How will the use of nonfiction reading clubs affect the reading comprehension of third-grade male students?
	How will explicit vocabulary instruction with the required core stories affect students' vocabulary growth?
	How would Peer-Assisted Literacy Strategies (PALS), in which the students learn to coach each other in letter sound knowledge, blending, and sight words, affect the academic and social progress of struggling readers?
	What will the impact be on our first-grade students' vocabulary acquisition of using the scientific investigation process, including hands-on experiments and scientific terminology?
	What happens when I put culturally relevant literature in the hands of my eighth-grade reluctant readers?

(Continued)

Figure 3.2 (Continued)

Subject Area/Type of Learner	Sample Inquiry Questions/Wonderings
Writing	How will the adventures of Flat Stanley increase writing motivation and scores with kindergarten and first-grade emotionally/behaviorally disordered students?
	How will the implementation of oral storytelling in writer's workshops affect my students' writing?
	What effect would daily blogging have on my high school juniors' writing?
Social Sciences	How do group projects affect academic outcomes in seventh-grade social studies?
	Given that there is a new standard that mandates the teaching of the Holocaust at every grade level, how can I deepen my adult-level knowledge about this part of our history, and how can I translate my newly acquired adult knowledge into pedagogically and developmentally appropriate lessons for the students I teach?
	What would be the impact of teaching specific nonfiction reading strategies during my world history class on the students passing my course?
	How will the participation in group service learning projects affect my students' attendance in economics class?
Mathematics	How will using a rubric to evaluate math partnership discussions enable struggling math students to have rich conversations about mathematics?
	In what ways will the systematic use and monitoring of math journals, where the emphasis is explaining "math moves," help my students grow as mathematicians?
	How will using problem-based learning of math concepts affect student achievement?
	What impact will diagnosing math difficulties and providing small group math-targeted lessons in computation, number sense, and problem solving have on sixth- and seventh-grade students' math achievement levels and attitude toward math?
	What is the impact on math achievement and attitudes of students using iPod Touches in mathematics?
Science	What is the effect of the Fifth-Grade After School Rocket Club on the attitudes of the fifth-grade students about science, math, and college as they enter into middle school?
	What impact will assigning a weekly family science investigation for homework have on science achievement?
	What is the effect of weekly guest speakers who are working in a science field on the attitudes of my ninth-grade biology students?
	What happens to my students' science scores when the eighth-grade reading teacher uses my science book to teach reading strategies?

Subject Area/Type of Learner	Sample Inquiry Questions/Wonderings
Art/Music	How can still life drawing help children see multiple perspectives and apply this to social situations?
	What is the relationship between students' expressing themselves through art and their writing for language arts assignments?
	Which music and movement techniques can help improve my students' behavior during large group/circle time?
	How can I teach music theory in a performance-oriented class?
Technology	How can a team of teachers work through problems together and support each other to overcome hurdles when using new technologies?
	How can I use a SMART Board to best facilitate student learning?
English Language Learners (ELL)	How does peer interaction facilitate an ELL's writing at the Kindergarten writing center?
	What is the impact of increasing student prosodic reading (especially pace, intonation, expression, and volume) on ELL students' achieving greater reading comprehension?
	What will be the impact on achievement of my ELL students when I use a consistent conferring routine during independent reading?
	What is the impact of implementing an extended intentional "Read Aloud" process on vocabulary acquisition of ELL middle grade students?
Social, Emotional, and Behavioral Supports	What is the relationship between implementing weekly, noncontingent physical education/social skills lessons with students who exhibit inappropriate school behavior and their ability to remain in regular education classes?
	How will early, positive, but ongoing parent connections affect student behavior and performance?
	In what ways will four-way team teaching in fifth grade provide a better transition into middle school?
	How can our understanding of cultural differences affect what happens in the classroom?
	What is the effect on the culture of teacher collaboration of working together on a community project and displaying photographs of each other demonstrating positive behaviors during this work?
	What effect will having tenth graders tutor younger students have on their feeling about the importance of school?
	How does the development and implementation of a Behavior Support Team affect school culture and teacher satisfaction?
	How does a schoolwide discipline plan affect the culture of the school?
	How does emotionally/behaviorally disordered students' involvement in the arts encourage the development of empathy?

WHAT ARE THE BENEFITS OF
INQUIRY-ORIENTED LEARNING COMMUNITIES?

There are many benefits for teachers who engage in inquiry-oriented learning community work. We'll describe four major benefits here, but they are like large stones dropped into water that create many smaller reverberations.

1. Reduced Isolation. First, just like their principals who collaborate in a professional learning community, teachers who become members of an inquiry-oriented PLC reduce their feelings of isolation from other adults. Teaching has long been and continues to be a profession that is plagued, for the most part, by isolation. Roland Barth (1990) writes,

> I do not think that teachers and principals really like to work the greater part of each day swamped by students and isolated from adults, secluded in what one teacher called "our adjoining caves." I do not believe that teachers or principals really teach or learn well in a climate of competition, isolation, or siege. Rather, I believe that one high school teacher speaks for most in saying, "I don't want to get out. I want to get better at what I do along with others who are equally interested in their personal and professional growth." (p. 33)

This is exactly what engagement in inquiry-oriented PLCs accomplishes: It helps teachers get better at what they do along with others equally interested in personal and professional growth.

2. Shared Purpose. Once teachers join each other in inquiry-oriented PLC work, collaboration in and of itself confers a huge benefit. Hunter, Bailey, and Taylor (1995) suggest that when it comes to collaboration, "One + one + one + one = Five" (p. 26). This unconventional equation is what happens when teachers work together toward a common objective: They arrive at a better understanding of student learning and instructional practices that support student learning. The PLCs become self-organizing systems that generate learning, which increases the productivity of the members of the PLC and of the PLC itself (Putnam, 1995). When people work together, they create synergy that helps move the group toward fulfilling a shared purpose.

3. Real Conversations. This synergy of shared purpose is often a byproduct of "ramping up" the dialogue and conversation that occurs between teachers in the school. According to Peter Senge (2007), developing capabilities for real conversation in schools is not easy.

Most of what passes for conversation in contemporary society is more like a Ping-Pong game than true talking and thinking together. Each individual tosses his or her view at the other. Each then responds. Often, we are preparing our response before we have even heard the other person's view. In effect, we are "taking our shot" before we have even received the other's ball. "Learningful" conversations require individuals capable of reflecting on their own thinking.

For this reason, we recommend strongly that PLCs structure their conversations using protocols (see, e.g., http://nsrfharmony.org/protocols.html). If protocols are not utilized to structure conversation, the dialogue can easily veer off topic, certain members of the group might dominate, and meeting time may run out before other members of the learning community get the opportunity to share their thinking. Using protocols ensures that "learningful" conversations will happen among teachers in a school.

4. Meaningful Data. A final benefit of inquiry-oriented learning community work is that it is driven by data. In today's schools data are *everywhere*, and teachers (and principals) can easily get lost or, as one teacher explained, "drown in data." When teachers engage in learning community work, they are constantly looking at data to inform their practice, but they have a mechanism for looking at data in a systematic way (inquiry). Rather than data becoming an unsystematic piling up of a bunch of numbers that are handed over to teachers (sometimes with punitive repercussions), data are thoughtfully collected and analyzed *for, with,* and *by* teachers in relation to inquiry questions. Engagement in inquiry-oriented learning community work ensures that all types of data (including student work, observations, interviews, video, pictures, reflective journals, blogs, and surveys) are analyzed alongside the most prevalent types of data available in schools today (standardized test scores, assessment measures, and grades). This ensures a healthy balance and marriage between formative data collection and summative data collection, as well as between quantitative and qualitative forms of data. In summary, engagement in inquiry-oriented learning community work helps teachers thrive in the sea of data, rather than drown.

WHAT ARE THE CHALLENGES OF INQUIRY-ORIENTED LEARNING COMMUNITY WORK?

There are two major challenges to be faced in inquiry work, and neither is insurmountable: trust and time. To actualize many of the benefits of inquiry-oriented learning community work, members of the group must trust each other. Building trust among a group of teachers who are used to working in isolation and who traditionally do not share freely what isn't working well for them is no small task. Teachers must feel secure enough in their PLC to bring *all* data—the good, the bad, and the ugly (Taylor, 2002). A part of the PLC's culture must be the willingness to take risks and share the "ugly" data as well as the more successful examples of student learning. This can only occur when the members of the learning community have formulated a deep trust in and respect for one another.

Another, perhaps greater, challenge to developing effective inquiry-oriented PLCs is the same one faced by principals who wish to engage in the PPLC work described in Chapter 1: time. Although the issue of time is ever present, there are a number of fine ideas that are being implemented across the nation to help identify opportunities for job-embedded teacher learning through inquiry. These ideas and practices can be sorted into six categories that help to organize creative uses of time and money (Yendol-Hoppey & Dana, 2010): restructured time, staff time, released time, purchased time, better used time, and technology time. Given that lack of time will likely be the first and largest challenge you will encounter, we end this section by describing each of these categories and illustrating how districts across the nation *are* finding time for this work.

1. Restructured Time. *Restructured time* refers to strategies for rearranging time within the teacher-contracted school day, for example,

- Early student release or late start for students (students are sent home early or arrive later one day a week or month).
- Add more and regularly scheduled professional development days to the school calendar.
- Provide teachers who work together with a common planning time every week.
- Extend the school day on four days of the week and dismiss early on the fifth day.
- Extract time from the existing schedule by taking a few minutes from each period to create an extra planning period for teachers.
- Block schedule to provide longer periods of release time for teachers (e.g., schedule electives like art and physical education back to back so that grade-level PLCs have a block of time to meet).
- Extend the school calendar to allow for a critical mass of professional development days at the beginning and end of the school year.

2. Staff Time. *Staff time* refers to strategies that alter the ways staff are utilized, for example,

- Make better use of the adults in the building who are not teachers (i.e., paraprofessionals, college interns, parents, community volunteers, and administrators). All these adults can be engaged with students on a regular basis in purposeful ways, to free up teachers to meet with one another during the school day. An underutilized source is the adult volunteer. To free teachers, create and train a volunteer pool that provides your school with more adults to disperse and utilize in creative ways.

- Institute "Specialist Days." Specialist days are full days when students rotate through their media, art, music, computer, and physical education specials for an entire day, freeing up time for classroom teachers to meet.

3. Released Time. Closely related to staff time, *released time* refers to strategies that release teachers from other responsibilities during the contracted school day so that they may engage in job-embedded professional learning, for example,

- Create a bank of substitute hours teachers could "cash in" to use for their professional development needs.
- Require all students to be involved in a certain number of community service hours over the course of a school year. While students are out earning community service hours, teachers can meet.
- Hire part-time permanent substitutes whose job is to rotate through the school, releasing teachers when needed to attend to professional development needs. Permanent substitutes ensure that continuous learning occurs even when the teacher of record leaves the classroom. A great and underutilized source of permanent substitutes is retired educators. Recruit retired educators for a permanent substitute pool.
- Develop an intentional, systematic extracurricular event or activity provided by the community so that students engage in a wide range of meaningful programming that supplements the curriculum while teachers work on school improvement.
- Create partner classrooms by teaming different subject area classes (in middle and high school) and different grade level classrooms (in elementary school). Teachers in partner classrooms take turns taking responsibility for a designated amount of time for the other teachers' classroom along with their own classroom, engaging in a meaningful curricular experience for the double-sized class of students. For example, middle school language arts and science teachers can team. The language arts teachers take the double class and engage the whole group in a creative writing activity about mitosis, the topic currently being taught by the science teacher, while the science teachers are released to meet with each other. The following week, the science teachers teach the double class, enacting the process of mitosis as a group dance, while the language arts teachers are released to meet with each other. In elementary school, the fifth-grade classrooms could partner with the kindergarten

classrooms. Each week, the kindergarten teachers and fifth-grade teachers alternate running a partner reading program in which fifth graders read to their kindergarten partner for 30 minutes right before lunch, freeing up either the fifth grade or kindergarten team to meet an hour each week over lunch (30 minutes reading time plus lunch time).

- Use large classes for special topics, create independent study for students, or occasionally substitute appropriate television or video programming for regular instruction.

4. Purchased Time. *Purchased time* refers to providing incentives for teachers to spend time outside the contractual day on job-embedded professional development. Payment for this extra time can cover weekends, afterschool, and summer work and may take the following forms:

- Money. A great place to reinvest some of the money a district can save by not relying on expensive educational consultants who come in to the district for a one-size-fits-all professional development workshop.
- Earning continuing certification hours needed for professional license renewal or graduate credits if a district partners with a college or university.
- Trading time (e.g., Working on a Saturday and getting the day before Thanksgiving off).
- Trading requirements (e.g., for tenured teachers, trading participation in the annual observation/conference/evaluation cycle with the administrator for a more meaningful completion of one cycle through the inquiry process that captures evidence related to the teacher and his or her students' growth over the course of the school year).

5. Better Used Time. *Better used time* refers to strategies for reconceptualizing existing meetings that may not be utilized to their fullest potential, for example,

- Faculty meetings. Rather than the administrator utilizing the bulk of meeting time to make announcements, the administrator takes care of announcements through e-mails and newsletters, and faculty meeting time is replaced with learning community meeting time.
- The grade-level team meeting (in elementary and middle schools) and the department meeting (in high schools). In many schools, the time during these meetings is sometimes taken up with congenial conversation or complaining sessions. Congenial conversations refer to the friendly, cordial dialogue that some teachers have with one another in the workplace. We see congeniality when teachers chat about weekend plans, last night's football game, or the latest episode of *American Idol*. Although schools

need congeniality, congeniality alone does not promote teacher learning and professional knowledge construction. Complaining sessions are times that teachers vent about difficulties they may be experiencing with individual students or classes or requirements from the school administration, district administration, or state. Although venting is sometimes a necessary release for the stresses associated with teaching, complaint sessions generally never solve problems, and they may even contribute to plummeting morale. Scrutinize the ways grade level and department meeting time is currently being utilized in a school to assess whether too much time is spent on congenial conversation in lieu of collegial learning or conversation gets stuck in a cycle of complaint. Work to replace congenial and complaint conversation time with grade level or department team meetings that function as inquiry-oriented learning communities.

- Teacher work days. Many districts have two to four professional development days scheduled throughout the year, when students have a holiday while teachers work. Often, these professional development days are conceptualized as the one-shot workshop. Rather than fill all these days with workshops, use some of them for learning community meetings and, at the end of a school year, allow teachers to share the results of the inquiry they've engaged in throughout the year.

6. Technology Time. *Technology time* refers to utilizing some of the latest technology to make it easier for teachers to meet and engage in professional discussion and learning. For example, it is often easier for teachers to meet and converse with one another in an asynchronous fashion than it is to meet face to face. It is often also easier for teachers from different schools in the same district to meet virtually rather than face to face, to save travel time. Asynchronous conversation and virtual meetings can be accomplished through the following:

- Online discussion forums;
- Blogging, Twittering, and Facebook groups; and
- Video conferencing.

How Can You Make Inquiry-Oriented Learning Communities Happen in Your District?

The suggestions for finding time listed in the previous section are helpful as a general framework for implementing inquiry-oriented learning community work. Examples of the creative ways in which schools and districts have fit inquiry work into their schedules are described in this section.

Sunset Hills Elementary. Principal Art Stuellet at Sunset Hills Elementary School in Tarpon Springs, FL organized his grade-level teams as inquiry-oriented learning communities; each team is charged with conducting a shared inquiry each school year. For example, during the 2009–2010 school year, his grade-level teams engaged in inquiry to explore the following questions:

- Kindergarten: What will be the effect of writing celebrations on student motivation and writing proficiency?
- First Grade: What happens when we engage in systematic conferring with our students, maintaining and using conferring notes on students' reading habits?
- Second Grade: What impact will implementing the science curriculum using the five E's (explore, explain, engage, expand, elaborate) have on students' interest and engagement in science?
- Third Grade: How will using math journals and teacher-created jingles affect students' understanding of math multiples and math factors?
- Fourth Grade: What impact will using literature to teach students to read like writers have on students' ability to produce writing pieces that are detailed and paint a picture with words?
- Fifth Grade: How will the implementation of book clubs affect students reading habits and skills?
- Physical Education: What effect will incorporating reading strategies into PE classes have on the academic performance of struggling students?
- Guidance: What impact will teaching peer conflict resolution have on the incidents of bullying in fourth and fifth grade?
- ESOL (English for Speakers of Other Languages): What impact will a student-created "portable" word wall have on the acquisition of sight and vocabulary words for first grade ESOL students?

> Sunset Hills Elementary found time for its teachers to engage in inquiry-oriented learning community work by reconceptualizing grade-level team meetings.

At the end of the school year, Principal Stuellet devoted a faculty meeting to his teachers' sharing their learning through inquiry with one another; he created a printed program to document the adult learning that occurred in his school that year. He had tee shirts printed for every faculty member with the Sunset Hills logo on the front and a big question mark on the back with the slogan "Inquiring Minds Want to Know and Grow" (see Figure 3.3). He had a picture taken of his entire faculty wearing their inquiry tee shirts, and he placed this photo on the cover of the program for the inquiry-sharing faculty meeting.

Figure 3.3 Inquiry T-Shirts

Union County Public Schools. Union County Public Schools is a small, rural district in Florida consisting of only three schools—one elementary, one middle, and one high school. The schools were members of an inquiry initiative as part of their membership in the North East Florida Educational Consortium (NEFEC), a consortium of 16 rural school districts in the state. The Union County reading coach, Rhonda Clyatt, took on the responsibility of serving as the district's

> Union County Schools found time and resources for its teachers to engage in inquiry-oriented learning community work by creating incentives for teachers to earn PD points and utilizing an early release day to share the results of their learning through inquiry districtwide.

inquiry coach as well. Teachers in Union County were presented with the option of participating in an inquiry-oriented learning community facilitated by Rhonda. The learning communities met approximately once a month after school for 60 to 90 minutes. During each meeting, Rhonda facilitated the participating teachers in designing and conducting individual inquiries into their practice. Each monthly meeting focused on a different topic: Introduction to Inquiry, Developing Your Wondering, Data Collection and Developing an Inquiry Plan, Analyzing Data, Using Literature to Support Your Work, and Sharing Your Work with Others. Teachers who agreed to participate and completed the inquiry process were awarded a substantial number of "professional development points" needed to renew their Florida teaching license every five years. In addition, Rhonda organized a districtwide inquiry showcase at the end of the school year, to give all Union County inquirers the opportunity to share their learning with each other and other teachers and administrators in the district. The showcase was held on an early release day. Students went home at noon, and teachers and administrators stayed through the afternoon to attend and participate in the showcase.

> The State College Area School District found time and resources for its teachers to engage in inquiry-oriented learning community work by reconceptualizing faculty meetings and allowing tenured teachers to opt for inquiry in lieu of a traditional observation and evaluation done by the principal.

The State College Area School District. The State College Area School District in State College, PA introduced inquiry into the school district in the early 1990s as part of a professional development school partnership with The Pennsylvania State University. Originally, the majority of the inquiry work that was being done in the school district was conducted by preservice teachers (Dana, Silva, & Snow-Gerono, 2002), but it didn't take long for the district to realize the power inquiry held for their veteran teachers as well. Once teachers were tenured in the district, they were up for a formal evaluation by their administrator every three years. To provide incentive for teachers to engage in inquiry, the district began offering tenured teachers the option of participating in an inquiry-oriented learning community and sharing the results at an annual district inquiry conference in the spring, instead of being formally evaluated. One State College Area School District principal, Donnan Stoicovy, took the district-provided incentive for her teachers to engage in the process of inquiry one step further. She reconceptualized the monthly faculty meetings at her school to create the time for teachers to meet in small learning communities and discuss their inquiry work (Stoicovy, Burns, Ciuffetelli, & Harris, 2009). At the end of each faculty meeting, teachers would reflect, in writing, on their work in small groups for that day. Stoicovy utilized these reflections to better understand the ways she could scaffold her teachers' learning and obtain resources her teachers needed to continue their inquiry work.

Fairfax County Schools. The Fairfax County School System in Virginia has a long, rich history of being innovative with the process of teacher research as one mechanism for their teachers' professional development, providing centrally funded release time for teachers to meet in their inquiry-oriented learning communities and holding a spring conference every year for teachers to share their work. The 2011 conference marked the 20th year Fairfax has held this event. Although sharing at

> Fairfax County Public Schools found time through technology for teachers to make public and share their learning through inquiry with one another.

this annual venue was always a highlight for all the Fairfax County teacher inquirers, the teachers wished the sharing of their inquiries wasn't confined to the spring conference. They yearned for more opportunities to learn from each others' research. Hence, to spread learning through inquiry throughout the district, Fairfax County created an in-house database that educators could access 24 hours a day, 7 days a week, 365 days a year.

What Role Does the Establishment of Inquiry-Oriented Learning Communities Play in a Districtwide Professional Development Program?

PLCs are an effective way to maximize professional development. Darling-Hammond and McLaughlin (1995) have argued that the professional development potential of PLCs can move educators beyond the acquisition of new knowledge and skills and help them rethink and reinvent instructional practices. The essential characteristics of these PLCs—shared values and norms, a clear and consistent focus on student learning, reflective dialogue, deprivatizing teaching practices, and a focus on collaboration—create a fundamental paradigm shift in the existing institutional structures of schools (DuFour, 2004; Louis & Marks, 1998).

Where Can I Learn More About Teacher Inquiry and Inquiry-Oriented Learning Communities?

• Whitford, B. L., & Wood, D. R. (2010). *Teachers learning in community: Realities and possibilities.* Albany: State University of New York Press. This book summarizes and synthesizes the culmination of six years of research in five states on professional learning communities. The realities of establishing and maintaining effective inquiry-oriented learning communities are explored, coupled with powerful descriptions of effective learning communities.

- Dana, N. F., & Yendol-Hoppey, D. (2009). *The reflective educator's guide to classroom research: Learning to teach and teaching to learn through practitioner inquiry* (2nd ed.). Thousand Oaks, CA: Corwin. This book takes teachers step-by-step through each component of the inquiry process, from finding your wondering to analyzing data and sharing your work with others. The text elaborates in great detail on many of the concepts introduced in this chapter. Many examples of teachers' inquiries are shared.

- Dana, N. F., & Yendol-Hoppey, D. (2008). *The reflective educator's guide to professional development: Coaching inquiry-oriented learning communities.* While the focus of this book is on coaching, this text defines and explicates the inquiry-oriented learning community, containing a chapter that discusses 10 essential elements of healthy learning communities and many examples of how inquiry-oriented learning communities play out in practice.

REVIEW AND LOOKING AHEAD

In this chapter, we

1. defined the inquiry-oriented learning community,

2. discussed the benefits and challenges of this work for teachers,

3. suggested ways you can make inquiry-oriented learning communities happen in your district,

4. reviewed the role these communities of teachers play in the district-wide professional development program, and

5. suggested additional resources for learning more about teacher inquiry and the power of teachers learning in community.

In Chapter 4, we will illustrate the ways learning community work can play out in a school over the course of an entire year, using the story of Village Oaks Elementary School in Collier County, Florida and the work of one reading coach and four teachers who affectionately referred to their inquiry-oriented learning community as "The GIRLS"—Guiders of Instructional and Reflective Learning Strategies.

4

An Inquiry-Oriented PLC in Practice

The Story of the GIRLS

Systems successful in improving student learning are characterized by articulated norms and values, a focus on student learning, reflective dialogue, collaborative practice, and deprivatization of teaching.

—Garmston (2007)

After 25 years as a teacher, Kathy was one of approximately 200 teachers in her state to be named to a new position, reading coach, as a part of a statewide initiative to improve reading and literacy in 2003. Kathy referred fondly to the Village Oaks Elementary School in Immokalee, Florida—where she had taught since its opening in 1987 and would now serve as reading coach—as "home." Nestled in southwest Florida, 40 miles from Naples, the Immokalee community of 30,000 permanent residents is a unique combination of Mexican, Guatemalan, and Haitian cultural traditions and heritages. Cattle and agriculture were the foundation of the early community, and seasonal farm workers are still vital to the area. At Village Oaks Elementary, one of six Immokalee elementary schools, the most common home language is Spanish, and there are growing numbers of Haitian Creole, Mam, Qanjobal, Mixtec, and Nahuatl speakers. Of the 600 students in this preK–6 school, almost half are migrants, 75% live in homes where a language other than English is spoken, and 97% of students are eligible for free breakfast and lunch. In recent years, the county school district has renovated Immokalee schools, providing current materials and technology as well as working to implement the latest research on teacher professional development, in an effort to target and improve the educational opportunities for Immokalee students.

When Kathy was in her third year as reading coach, inquiry was introduced to the Village Oaks faculty by a district professional development specialist who began a pilot program of inquiry to explore the potential of this form of professional learning for Immokalee teachers. During that pilot year, 14 teachers at Kathy's school engaged in inquiry and organized an "Inquiry Expo" held in one of the school's planning rooms where teachers shared their work with one another. Over time, inquiry as a powerful mechanism for professional development spread throughout her school and community, eventually leading to all schools in Immokalee establishing inquiry as a tool to enhance teacher quality and student achievement. During this time, Kathy combined the coaching of inquiry with her responsibilities as reading coach. Inquiry became a tool to engage teachers in thoughtful professional conversation, deep analysis of practice based on student work, and informed changes in practice to improve student learning.

At the start of the new school year, four of Kathy's teaching colleagues decided to meet as a cross-grade level PLC; they asked Kathy to facilitate their meetings and their engagement in inquiry. As Kathy was well liked and respected among her peers and widely perceived as a resource on reading research, data-driven decision making, state initiatives, and the uses and purposes of assessment tools, she was ready to "hit the ground running" with the inquiry work immediately. To kick off the year and provide incentives for these teachers to continue to meet and work together even during the busiest times of the year, Kathy arranged for each member of this cross-grade level inquiry-oriented PLC to earn professional development points toward recertification from these meetings. Some meetings would be during contract hours (early release days) while other meetings would take place after contract hours. As one teacher said, "They are not mandated by our principal. These are meetings initiated by teachers for teachers."

> "These are meetings initiated by teachers for teachers."

Having dubbed themselves "The GIRLS" (Guiders of Instructional and Reflective Learning Strategies), this PLC, composed of kindergarten teacher Tracey, first-grade teacher Alicia, second-grade teacher Sheila, and third-grade teacher Debbie, was ready to begin inquiry.

SEPTEMBER

Establishing the Foundation for The GIRLS' Work Together

The Creating Metaphors Protocol

Knowing the importance of building trust, Kathy began this group's initial meeting with a National School Reform Faculty protocol to help the teachers open up to each other about professional challenges as well as make discoveries about their identities as teachers by composing and sharing a metaphor that describes their teaching.

Kathy reviewed the steps to the "Creating Metaphors" protocol (http://nsrfharmony.org/protocol/doc/creating_metaphors.pdf): First, each teacher completed the statement, "When I am at my best as a teacher, I am _____." Next, the teacher drew a picture, symbol, or some other graphic representation of the metaphor she selected to complete the statement. Each person also jotted down a few sentences to describe the guidance this metaphor offers in sticky situations as well as to reflect on the "shadows" inherent in her metaphor.

When everyone in the group had finished, Tracey, Alicia, Sheila, Debbie, and Kathy shared their metaphors with one another. Tracey volunteered to speak first: "I am a surfer, always awake to the hazards, but excited and enjoying life. I ride the waves of the classroom with all the ups and downs. No matter how out of control it gets, I always go back for more in search of that perfect ride." Debbie joined in, "I am an astronaut. My students and I have different types of knowledge and we must work as a team on the mission of learning and discovering. Like a mission, sometimes my students lead, sometimes I chart our course, and sometimes we get 'lost in space' as we attempt to go where no one has ever gone before."

After the remaining members of the learning community shared their metaphors, Kathy asked each learning community member to discuss both the strengths and shadows of each metaphor in turn. After a learning community member's metaphor was discussed by the group, Kathy returned the conversation to the teacher who presented the metaphor and asked her to discuss what parts of the strengths/shadows discussion resonated with her teaching experience. After all metaphors had been presented and discussed, Kathy debriefed the activity in two steps: She asked them to talk about what they learned about each other and how they might do something similar with their students. Although these women were good and congenial friends, Kathy knew they were venturing into a new professional relationship as they established an inquiry-oriented PLC. Kathy's immediate goal for utilizing this metaphor activity during the initial meeting was to reinforce the mutual trust these teachers felt while refocusing their relationship around professional issues.

Following the metaphor activity, the group established the norms for their PLC. The conversation around establishing norms began with Kathy reviewing some suggested norms she had already written on chart paper:

- Speak from the heart.
- Monitor equity of participation.
- Acknowledge each other as equals.
- Assume goodwill.
- Trust the process.
- Expect it to get messy at times.

After briefly explaining each norm, Kathy addressed the group: "These are some suggestions based on norms I have found useful in my coaching. Is there anything on this list that you don't agree with for our learning community or anything that you'd like to add?" Alicia suggested, "We teach in a small community where everyone knows all about everyone. We need to be able to talk openly without fear that our words will be repeated anywhere. We have to agree that what we say in these meetings stays in these meetings." All of the teachers nodded in agreement, and Kathy smiled as she added the words "Vegas Rules" to their chart, chuckling aloud, "You know that old saying, 'What happens in Vegas stays in Vegas.' Well, we can't afford a trip to Vegas, but we can use that saying to remind us that what we share about ourselves, our teaching, and our students does not get discussed anywhere other than in our meetings. 'Vegas Rules' is code for 'What happens in our PLC stays in our PLC.'"

> "Q-TIP stands for 'Quit Taking It Personally.'"

Sheila offered another suggestion: "Since we're talking code here, could we add another one? How about Q-TIP? Q-TIP stands for 'Quit taking it personally.' This ground rule was established in my PLC last year, and I think it's pretty important. Because we all know each other well, conversations can easily veer from professional to personal within the same sentence. Q-TIP will remind us that our work during these meetings is about student and teacher learning—it is not about anyone's personality or behavior." All the teachers nodded their heads in agreement, and the group was ready to begin thinking about inquiry.

Kathy said, "Alright, now that we've analyzed our teaching with metaphors and established some ground rules for our work together, it's time to get to the heart of our first meeting. When you invited me to facilitate your meetings this year, you said that you have all found inquiry to be a powerful form of professional development in the past, and you wanted to try working cross-grade levels this year to investigate an issue at multiple levels. One of the components of the inquiry process that is most critical to its success in teacher professional development is that the teacher inquirer is in charge of her learning and is passionate about what she is studying. So today, let's utilize the bulk of our time together to discuss our passions and our dilemmas—what keeps us up at night or what we think about as we drive to and from our school every day. By spending some time in this discussion, we can explore where everyone would like to focus their inquiry work this year. Sound OK to everyone?"

The Passion Profiles Protocol

The teachers once again nodded in agreement, and Kathy led the teachers through another NSRF protocol, "Passion Profiles Activity" (http://nsrfharmony.org/protocol/doc/passion_profiles_activity.pdf).

In this protocol, each teacher selects one of eight passions related to inquiry that she most closely identifies with: the student, the curriculum, specific content knowledge, teaching strategies, the relationship between beliefs and practice, the relationship between personal and professional identities, social justice issues, or the importance of context (see Figure 4.1).

Figure 4.1 Passion Profiles

Passion 1: The Child

You became a teacher primarily because you wanted to make a difference in the life of a child. Perhaps you were one of those whose life was changed by a committed, caring teacher, and you decided to become a teacher so that you could do that for other children. You are always curious about particular students whose work and/or behavior just doesn't seem to be in sync with the rest of the students in your class. You often wonder about how peer interactions seem to affect a student's likelihood to complete assignments, or what enabled one of your ELL students to make such remarkable progress seemingly overnight, or how to motivate a particular student to get into the habit of writing. You believe that understanding the unique qualities that each student brings to your class is the key to unlocking his or her full potential as learners.

Passion 2: The Curriculum

You are one of those teachers who is always "tinkering" with the curriculum in order to enrich the learning opportunities for your students. You have a thorough understanding of your content area. You attend conferences and subscribe to journals that help you to stay current with trends affecting the curriculum that you teach. Although you are often dissatisfied with "what is" with respect to the prescribed curriculum in your school or district, you are almost always sure that you could do it better than the frameworks. You are always critiquing the existing curriculum and finding ways to make it better for the kids you teach—especially when you have a strong hunch that "there is a better way to do this."

(Continued)

Figure 1.1 (Continued)

Passion 3: Content Knowledge

You are at your best in the classroom when you have a thorough understanding of the content and/or topic you are teaching. Having to teach something you don't know much about makes you uncomfortable and always motivates you to hone that area of your teaching knowledge base. You realize that what you know about what you are teaching will influence how you get it across to your students in a developmentally appropriate way. You spend a considerable amount of your personal time—both during the school year and in the summer—looking for books, material, workshops, and courses you can take that will strengthen your content knowledge.

Passion 4: Teaching Strategies

You are motivated most by a desire to improve on and experiment with teaching strategies and techniques. You have experienced and understand the value of particular strategies to engage students in powerful learning and want to get really good at this stuff. Although you have become really comfortable with using cooperative learning with your students, there are many other strategies and techniques that interest you and that you want to incorporate into your teaching repertoire.

Passion 5: The Relationship Between Beliefs and Professional Practice

You sense a "disconnect" between what you believe and what actually happens in your classroom and/or school. For example, you believe that a major purpose of schools is to produce citizens capable of contributing to and sustaining a democratic society; however, students in your class seldom get an opportunity to discuss controversial issues because you fear that the students you teach may not be ready and/or capable of this, and you are concerned about losing control of the class.

Passion 6: The Intersection Between Your Personal and Professional Identities

You came into teaching from a previous career and often sense that your previous identity may be in conflict with your new identity as an educator. You feel ineffective and frustrated when your students or colleagues don't approach a particular task that is second nature to you because of your previous identity—writer, actor, artist, researcher—in the same way that you do. What keeps you up at night is how to use the knowledge, skills, and experiences you bring from your previous life to make powerful teaching and learning happen in your classroom and/or school.

Passion 7: Advocating Equity and Social Justice

You became an educator to change the world—to help create a more just, equitable, democratic, and peaceful planet. You are constantly thinking of ways to integrate issues of race, class, disability, power, and so on into your teaching; however, your global concerns for equity and social justice sometimes get in the way of your effectiveness as an educator—like the backlash that resulted from the time you showed *Shindler's List* to your sixth-grade class. You know there are more developmentally appropriate ways to infuse difficult and complex issues into your teaching, and you want to learn more about how to do this with your students.

Passion 8: Context Matters

What keeps you up at night is how to keep students focused on learning despite the many daily disruptions in your classroom and building. It seems that the school context conspires against everything that you know about teaching and learning: adults who don't model the behaviors they want to see reflected in the students; policies that are in conflict with the schools mission; and above all, a high-stakes testing environment that tends to restrain the kind of teaching and learning that you know really works for the students you teach.

Each person writes a few lines describing how she perceives herself in relation to her chosen passion. Then, people talk about the issues related to each passion that worry them. For example, concerning the passion "individual students," Debbie offered, "I am worried about specific students in my class who may have trouble passing the high stakes test this year." Regarding the social justice passion, Tracey expressed her concern about equity: "I worry about the gap between my kindergarteners who attended preK and those who did not." As the end of the meeting drew near, Kathy said, "Over the next few weeks, as you work with your kids, continue to think about your passions, your dilemmas, and your worries. Keep track of any questions that thinking about your passions, dilemmas, and worries generate for you, so we can discuss them at our next meeting. Thanks to everyone for a great start to our learning community work today. I can tell we are all going to learn a great deal."

OCTOBER THROUGH DECEMBER

Exploring Dilemmas and Questions

The Check-in Circle Activity

As a warm-up to discussing their dilemmas and questions, Kathy began the next meeting with a team-building activity called "Check-in Circle." This is a round-robin activity. Each person shares briefly how she is feeling at the moment. Hardly able to contain her excitement at what she was about to say, Alicia volunteered to go first. "I'm feeling triumphant—one of my students who came in August from Guatemala participated orally in class today for the first time!" Alicia's comment elicited a variety of simultaneous "That's great!" comments and spontaneous applause by the group. Debbie went next. "I'm happy about your student, Alicia. Wish I had a similar teaching triumph to share today. Rather, I want to express a worry. One of my kiddos seems so fearful lately, particularly at the end of the day when it's time to go home. I'm concerned he might be getting bullied by bigger kids on the bus." The mood of the collective response shifted from elation in response to Alicia to supportive comments for Debbie. After the remaining members of the group took a turn sharing their feelings, Kathy brought this short opening activity to a close by thanking everyone for checking in and reviewing the agreed-upon norms. Then Kathy turned the attention to the dilemmas and questions they had been asked to think about since the previous meeting. Once again, Alicia volunteered to go first. "I've been thinking quite a bit about vocabulary. My first graders are struggling with specialized words that they need for different content areas. I want to help them but I'm not sure how." Kathy responded, "That's a wonderful reason for us to do a consultancy about vocabulary."

The Consultancy Protocol

The teachers in the group were all familiar with the "Consultancy Protocol" and often used it to help each other clarify their thinking (http://nsrfharmony.org/protocol/doc/consultancy.pdf). The group agreed to do a consultancy with Alicia and followed the steps of the protocol:

1. Alicia summarized the dilemma that was bothering her. Virtually all the students at Village Oaks Elementary lived in homes where a language other than English was spoken. Although the students had learned English early and became fluent quickly, their English vocabulary scores indicated that they had not mastered "academic" vocabulary—the specialized vocabulary used in content classes. This vocabulary includes terms such as *calculate, contrast, genre,* and *nonfiction,* as well as common terms with specialized meaning, like *table, field,* and *scale.* Alicia wanted to do something different to help her students, but she didn't know what to do.

2. The members of the learning community asked Alicia clarifying questions, which are questions that have simple, factual answers and provide information the group needs to know to understand the dilemma. For example, Tracey asked whether Alicia saw the same issue in all content areas or it was more pronounced in one discipline. Alicia responded that science vocabulary seemed to be the most challenging for her students.

3. The members of the learning community asked Alicia probing questions, which are open-ended questions that are designed to help Alicia dig deeper into her thinking. For example, Sheila asked Alicia what she believed to be the root of the problem with science vocabulary: finding specific vocabulary strategies that might help students, questioning the appropriateness of the whole first-grade science curriculum, or some other foundational issue. After some thought, Alicia responded that she believed exploring different strategies to build science vocabulary might be useful.

4. Alicia pulled her chair back, remained silent, and took notes while the others discussed her dilemma as if she weren't in the room. Debbie pointed out that the science curriculum is organized abstractly, with vocabulary and

discussions of the scientific method often presented in isolation. However, the students live in a farming community; many of the parents work in agriculture and do a lot of applied science. Many mothers prepare traditional meals from scratch—more applied science. Could Alicia involve parents in demonstrating some hands-on science to the students, which Alicia could then connect to the scientific vocabulary that students needed to learn?

5. Alicia rejoined the group, consulted her notes, and summarized for the group how her thinking about her dilemma changed after listening to their discussion. As a result of the consultancy, Alicia planned to focus her inquiry on science vocabulary and the question, "What is the relationship between bringing parents in to demonstrate hands-on science (which I will then tie explicitly to scientific vocabulary and the scientific method) and my students' acquisition and understanding of scientific vocabulary?"

At the end of Step 5, Kathy debriefed the consultancy by thanking Alicia for sharing and posing the following questions to the group: "How did following the steps of the consultancy protocol help us to communicate effectively and efficiently?" and "What, if any, impact did this consultancy have on your thought processes?" Alicia immediately responded, "I would not have arrived at a working question so quickly without the group input." Sheila added, "I never would have thought about bringing in parents for science instruction. That was such a great idea from Debbie. I think I'd like to explore the possibility of doing the same thing in my second-grade classroom." The meeting ended with the teachers conferring about ways they might modify the consultancy protocol so that their students could use it to sharpen their thinking.

During the November and December meetings, the teachers used consultancies to address other members' dilemmas. At the end of the November meeting, the group decided that they wished to engage in *intersecting* inquiry in which all members of the learning community explore subquestions related to an overarching topic.

Because Village Oaks had the lowest science scores in the county during the previous testing cycle, everyone agreed to work on science vocabulary acquisition, but each teacher had her own dilemma or wondering.

> . . . everyone agreed to work on science vocabulary acquisition. . . .

Alicia decided to explore her original idea to study the impact of showcasing parents' applied science expertise on students' mastery of science vocabulary. Debbie decided to look at how increased student engagement resulting from participation in hands-on science experiments affects mastery of scientific vocabulary. Sheila decided to use science centers, each with a different focus, to differentiate science instruction by student interest. Her students would choose which center they would work in. In addition to hands-on experiments, each center would include work on basic scientific vocabulary. As reading coach, Kathy decided to collaborate with Roy, a fourth-grade teacher, to implement thematic instruction with a science focus. She wondered what would be the outcome of reading and writing about science exploration, science discoveries, and biographies of famous scientists during the language arts block, while carrying out related science experiments during another period of the day. Each teacher's wondering was couched in terms of studying the impact of an innovation related to the acquisition of science vocabulary in a specific classroom.

By the holiday break, the teachers were ready to begin their inquiries. Kathy reminded them that reading and research was an essential component of the inquiry process, to establish a foundation for their innovation before implementing significant changes in their classrooms. The group brainstormed possible resources for their work, including electronic reading and science journals, the teacher's guide for the science textbook series, the school science coach, the district supervisor of science instruction, and a professor one of them had during her undergraduate studies. Each member of the PLC chose a resource to investigate and report on at their next meeting after they returned from the winter holiday break.

JANUARY AND FEBRUARY

Individual Work

During January and February, the PLC members formulated individual data collection plans, organized their thinking, and shared their preliminary research results. All the teachers included both quantitative data (such as assessment measures of science vocabulary) and qualitative data (such as observations of students, interviews with students, attendance records, and parent feedback). Each teacher implemented her inquiry plan soon after the December break. During the winter months, meetings were less structured; they were held in response to expressed needs of a teacher, and not everyone was able to attend every meeting. However, Kathy, in her capacity as reading coach, was in frequent communication with all members of the PLC and provided individual support as appropriate.

MARCH

Data Analysis

The Data-Driven Dialogue Protocol

In March, the entire PLC had a lengthy meeting to begin to analyze their data sets using the "Data-Driven Dialogue" protocol (http://nsrfharmony .org/protocol/doc/data_driven_dialogue.pdf). To model the process,

Kathy went first: "I brought several pieces of data from my inquiry to share with you all today. I have student quizzes on science vocabulary dating from December through the end of February. I also brought the planning sheets that I co-constructed with Roy, the fourth-grade teacher, to highlight the scientific vocabulary that appeared in the books students read, in the writing prompts we provided, and also in the science work that the students did in class. Finally, I brought my anecdotal notes from the classroom. Now, let's follow each step of the protocol to examine these data in a systematic and careful way." The group proceeded through the following three steps:

1. Predictions. Silently, the teachers read through and examined all the data Kathy brought. Once all members had finished reading, they offered predictions based on what they saw in the data. Debbie said, "I assume that the teacher explicitly taught these vocabulary items as well as having them appear in written contexts." Alicia wondered whether all the words appeared on the class word wall.

2. Observations. During this phase, the teachers drew no conclusions and made no inferences; they just stated observations. For example, Sheila pointed out that she counted 15 students' names, but there were 20 students in this classroom. Tracey observed that when she laid the quizzes out in chronological order, she saw a pattern of rising scores. Debbie read aloud from Kathy's anecdotal notes about improved student behavior and evidence of increased interest in science class.

3. Inferences. With observations clearly articulated, the group moved on to drawing conclusions and explaining what they had observed in the data, as well as identifying what additional data, if any, would help to confirm or refute their preliminary conclusions. Alicia returned to Sheila's earlier comments about student numbers, pointing out that this class had many parents who were migrant workers, and it was possible that only 15 (of 20) students had been in the class for the entire two months of the inquiry. The group recommended clarifying this issue before conclusions were drawn about the impact of the inquiry. Debbie wondered about oral vocabulary—whether the students use these words appropriately in class discussions. She didn't see any information about this in Kathy's anecdotal notes. She wished the teacher had included some anecdotal observations of students. Tracey pointed out that the teacher could still do something, such as interview the students and ask how they felt about this curricular innovation. The learning community members wrote up their inferences for Kathy to share and discuss with Roy, the classroom teacher she was collaborating with.

In summary, through use of this protocol, the learning community members observed patterns and drew conclusions by considering Kathy's data in a systematic way. At first, they concentrated on assessment data— had students increased their mastery of scientific terms?

Then they began to notice other interesting things: Student behavior improved in science class, students asked when they could work on their science experiments, and students seemed to have greater reading stamina when reading nonfiction books about science than they did when reading fiction.

At the end of the protocol, Kathy thanked the group. "Wow, thanks to your great thinking, I have a wonderful summary of things you noticed in the data that I can't wait to share with Roy. I am reminded of the power of protocols. Who would like to present their data next?"

One by one, Tracey, Alicia, Sheila, and Debbie presented their data for the learning community to work through using the same process. At the end of their meeting, the teachers all agreed they were exhausted by the intensity of the work but exhilarated to be learning so much about the complexity of teaching ESL students science vocabulary.

APRIL AND MAY

Polish and Present

In April, the PLC met to "polish up the work" for the community-wide Inquiry Expo. The PLC decided to present their work with one over-arching question: "How can we help our students master scientific vocabulary?" Each teacher designed a separate inquiry write-up and display board to share with interested educators. Each person brought her preliminary write-up to the April meeting. The teachers did a round-robin silent reading of all the write-ups. Each provided feedback to everyone else. They agreed to revise their write-ups independently.

In May, the PLC members presented their work at the Inquiry Expo, they wrote up their final report for inclusion on a district inquiry website, and they met to reflect on and celebrate their collective inquiry journey.

The GIRLS were excited to learn, when district science assessment scores were reported in June, that their students' science scores had improved significantly. They celebrated and eagerly began to discuss possible wonderings to explore next year. The inquiry-oriented learning community work had enabled this cross-grade level group of teachers to wrap their own professional learning around the learning of their students, and they couldn't wait to begin the cycle again.

QUESTIONS FOR DISCUSSION

Part II: For the Teacher

Part II of this text focused on the teacher's role in building a successful districtwide professional development plan. Reflect on Part II and apply what you've learned from the two chapters to your own context by answering the following questions:

1. The GIRLS began their learning community work by discussing metaphors that encapsulated their teaching practice, in order to get to know each other better and simultaneously focus their conversation on teaching and learning. What other activities might be utilized to help learning community members accomplish these two goals simultaneously?

2. In order to develop a question to guide their work, members of this learning community explored eight passions (Figure 4.1).

- Which of these eight passions is most important to you? Why?
- What potential inquiry questions might be generated from your classroom, school, or district based on each of the eight passions?

3. Two of the protocols the GIRLS used throughout their work were the consultancy protocol (to help define an inquiry question/wondering) and the data-driven dialogue protocol (to help teachers begin the process of data analysis).

- What value did these protocols add to the group meetings?
- In what ways might you use these protocols in your own district or school?

4. What do you feel would be the greatest benefit to establishing inquiry-oriented learning communities in your school or district?

5. What do you feel would be the greatest challenge to establishing inquiry-oriented learning communities in your school or district? How might these challenges be addressed?

PART III

The Student's Role

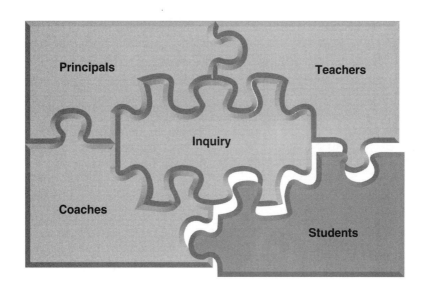

5

Introducing Inquiry Into the Classroom

Most people believe our schools' primary purpose is to prepare children for their future as workers, rather than to educate them to be complete human beings. This narrow aim of preparing children for employment means that our schools do not teach a love for learning, caring and empathy, moral consciousness, media literacy, social responsibility, ecological literacy, peace and nonviolence, creativity and imagination, intellectual curiosity, and global awareness. Rethinking curricula as inquiry is one of the best ways we can teach this essential knowledge and make content and skills infinitely more meaningful.

—Steven Wolk (2008, p. 116)

So far in this book, we have focused on the critical role inquiry can play in the continuous learning of the adults in a district—administrators and teachers. Through inquiry, adult learning flourishes. The process of inquiry is aligned with much of what we know about adult learning (see, e.g., Brookfield, 1992; Knowles, 1990; Mezirow, 2000). First, adults have *ownership* in and of their learning. No longer is their professional development something done *to* them *by* others. Rather, they control and participate in their learning. Second, because professionals begin the process of inquiry by articulating a burning question that emerges from a felt difficulty or dilemma in practice, by definition and design, the process of inquiry ensures that teachers' and administrators' learning is *immediate* and *relevant* to their lives and work as educators. Third, engagement in inquiry is *differentiated*. Not all teachers and administrators are learning exactly the same thing in exactly the same way at exactly the same time. Rather, inquiry establishes a path for learning to emerge for each educator based on his or her needs, prior knowledge and experiences, abilities, learning style, and current classroom and school context. Fourth, in large part, inquiry is *self-directed* as teachers and principals take initiative and responsibility for the design and implementation of the inquiry cycle— selecting a question that is relevant and meaningful to explore, managing data collection to gain insights into the question, and assessing their own learning through data analysis. Fifth, inquiry is *collaborative*. Teachers and principals discuss and critically reflect on practice together using mean- ingful and structured dialogue, collectively constructing knowledge about practice. Finally, the process of inquiry is *active* and *engaging.* Rather than passively participating in a "sit and get" workshop, educators learn from their own investigations as inquiry "turns traditional professional devel- opment on its head" (Check, 1997, p. 6).

In sum, inquiry enables the adults in the district to *own* their learning. In this chapter, we argue that inquiry is also a powerful form of learning for students. Just as it does for adult learners, engagement in inquiry makes student learning immediate, relevant, differentiated, self-directed, collaborative, active, and engaging. Here we introduce student inquiry as a strategy teachers can add to their pedagogical repertoire to enhance stu- dent learning at the classroom level.

What Is Student Inquiry?

Student inquiry is both a philosophy and an approach to the investigation- based organization of classroom learning. Students become researchers, writers, and activists rather than passive recipients of a textbook's content. Students take ownership of their learning; they discover that school can be a place that nurtures curiosity, inspires important questions, and produces real joy from learning.

In student inquiry, work is related to the life experiences of students; learners form their own questions, collect data, analyze their findings, and share their results with one another. Teachers scaffold their learners through a cycle:

1. Asking questions;

2. Investigating the questions through such mechanisms as library and Internet research, surveys, interviews, writing to e-pals in other countries, watching films, listening to music, and reading literature;

3. Creating something to show what the students found in their investigation;

4. Sharing what was created;

5. Reflecting on their work;

6. Possibly acting on inquiry; and

7. Asking more questions (Wolk, 2008).

Questioning lies at the heart of inquiry and drives the teaching and learning process.

This description of student inquiry replicates the process of teacher and administrator inquiry described in Parts I and II of this text. In fact, according to Steven Wolk (2008), who has written extensively about school as inquiry,

> Inquiry-based teaching is a profound change from business as usual. Inquiry-based teaching transforms the aims of school from short-term memorization of facts into disciplined questioning and investigating. . . . And inquiry-based schools at their very best also invite—even expect—teachers and administrators to use inquiry to improve their practice. In this sense, inquiry becomes far more than a pedagogical theory or a teaching method; it becomes a way of life inside school. (pp. 116–117)

Engaging students in inquiry enables powerful learning to become a way of life inside schools, not only for the administrators and the teachers, but for the students as well.

The emphasis on teaching as inquiry has been most prevalent in science. In fact, for years, the National Science Education Standards have articulated clearly the importance of students learning science content through inquiry:

> Students at all grade levels and in every domain of science should have the opportunity to use scientific inquiry and develop the ability to think and act in ways associated with inquiry, including asking questions, planning and conducting investigations, using appropriate tools and techniques to gather data, thinking critically and logically about relationships between evidence and explanations, constructing and analyzing alternative explanations, and communicating scientific arguments. (National Research Council, 1996, p. 105)

Science is not the only place where inquiry is appropriate; in fact, the process of inquiry can be utilized in the teaching of any discipline. In addition, engaging students in inquiry is a great way to organize cross-disciplinary instruction. Whether elementary or secondary students are learning science, mathematics, social studies, or language arts, inquiry is a powerful tool to add to the classroom teacher's pedagogical toolbox. With inquiry, students become authentic investigators and researchers.

Daniel Callison (1999) defines four levels of inquiry for students: controlled, guided, modeled, and free (see Figure 5.1). In *controlled inquiry*, the teacher chooses the topic and identifies the resources that students will use to answer their questions. Often, students will have a specific product that they are required to produce as evidence of learning. This type of inquiry is often found in the traditional science classroom, where all students are working on a defined experiment with a predictable outcome, despite the fact that national leaders in science education are pushing away from controlled inquiry toward guided, modeled, and free inquiry.

Figure 5.1   Four Levels of Student Inquiry

Four Levels of Student Inquiry (Callison, 1999)	
Controlled Inquiry	Teacher chooses topic and identifies resources students will use to answer questions.
Guided Inquiry	Students choose topic but are required to produce a specific product.
Modeled Inquiry	Students follow the lead of the teacher as the whole class and the teacher engage in one collective inquiry together.
Free Inquiry	Students choose their topic without reference to any prescribed content.

In *guided inquiry,* students have more freedom to choose, although they are still required to produce a specific product, such as a written report or oral presentation.

An example of guided inquiry comes from the fifth-grade classroom of Stephanie Whitaker in Florida. When her district underwent rezoning and her school received a large number of English language learners as students, Stephanie became the language arts teacher for a class of fifth-grade students who were either currently or previously enrolled in the ESOL program. Stephanie saw this assignment as a challenge and decided to team teach the language arts block with the ESOL resource teacher at her school, Sharon Earle. Together, they used guided inquiry to engage their ESOL students in learning about literary genres. They taught students about the various genres of fiction appropriate to their grade level, including fairy tales, fiction, historical fiction, fantasy, and legend. In small groups and guided by one of the teachers, students posed questions like, "How do authors help readers connect to a text?" "What tools does a reader need to make connections to a text?" and "How do illustrators decide what to draw and what medium to use?" Over several weeks, students researched the answers to their questions. They read multiple books and worked in small groups to develop action plans and lay out timelines (see Figure 5.2). As a final product, each student was required to write and illustrate a fictional book, demonstrating his or her understanding of the writer's craft by doing things like matching the setting to the story.

Figure 5.2   Student Wonderings and Action Plans

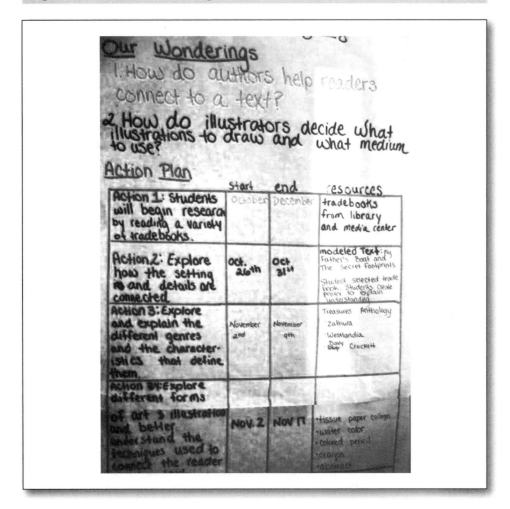

In *modeled inquiry*, students follow the lead of the teacher as the whole class and the teacher engage in one collective inquiry together. The teacher and students work side by side, learning together. Students have flexibility in topic choice and product.

A good example of modeled inquiry can be found in an elementary school in Maryland where students and teacher studied the annual migration of the monarch butterflies from Mexico to the U.S. (see Journey North: Children

> Practice Real Science by Monitoring Monarchs at http://www.edutopia.org/
> journey-north). Together the teacher and students studied the topic, with
> the teacher finding opportunities to address content standards (e.g., gram-
> mar and punctuation as children wrote letters to children in Mexico and
> scientific observation as students observed the emergence of a butterfly
> from a chrysalis).

Finally, in *free inquiry,* students choose their topic without reference to
any prescribed content.

> Two teachers from Tarpon Springs, Florida, Michele Morris and Dorie Sundholm,
> stumbled into utilizing free student inquiry almost by accident. When con-
> ducting their own inquiry into the effects of differentiated instruction in a
> classroom for gifted fourth graders, the two teachers focused on the ques-
> tion "How will curriculum compacting affect student performance?" They
> used the previous year's assessment results to determine which students
> had already mastered graphing. Those students were invited to conduct
> independent work. Much to the teachers' surprise, the students who did not
> need instruction in graphing decided to conduct their own inquiry related
> to classroom libraries in the school. The students explained that as strong
> readers, they often felt frustrated by what they perceived to be a relatively
> small collection of nonfiction books in their classrooms. Hence, they
> engaged in inquiry to systematically study the ratio of nonfiction to fiction
> books in each classroom, with the goal of better organizing reading selec-
> tions for all students and helping teachers and the librarian better
> understand the true nature of reading selections available to students. After
> visiting every classroom library and organizing and coding books as fiction
> or nonfiction, the students produced a group PowerPoint in which they
> applied the graphing skills they already had mastered to graph the ratio of
> fiction to nonfiction books in every classroom library in the school,
> grades K–5. This example of free inquiry revealed that almost every class-
> room had a much greater number of fiction books than nonfiction books.
> The students presented their inquiry results at a faculty meeting and then
> at a regional principals' meeting, making the case for the school librarian to
> purchase more nonfiction books for all classroom libraries.

WHAT ARE THE BENEFITS OF
INQUIRY FOR STUDENT LEARNING?

We opened this chapter by reviewing the reasons inquiry is a powerful
form of learning for adults: It makes learning *immediate, relevant, differentiated, self-directed, collaborative, active,* and *engaging.* By applying the funda-
mentals of teacher inquiry to student learning, teachers create a rich,
deeply intellectual environment in their classrooms that replicates all the

reasons inquiry is a powerful form of *adult* learning with *children* in elementary, middle, and high school classrooms.

In addition to the benefits already listed, an important purpose of inquiry-based instruction is to teach the skills of inquiry, including proficiency in the following:

- finding resources and doing traditional research;
- collecting and analyzing data;
- developing observation skills;
- interviewing and surveying;
- developing technical and creative writing skills;
- creating purposeful questions and hypotheses;
- utilizing computer skills;
- reading for information;
- designing science investigations; and
- developing aesthetic abilities and skill in discourse and argument.

These same skills are aligned with national standards that articulate clearly the needs of the 21st-century learner (International Society for Technology in Education, 2007; Partnership for 21st Century Skills, 2007). In particular, the National Educational Technology standards specify that students "apply digital tools to gather, evaluate, and use information" as well as "use critical thinking skills to plan and conduct research, manage projects, solve problems, and make informed decisions using appropriate digital tools and resources" (International Society for Technology in Education, 2007, p. 1). Hence, an additional benefit of applying the tenets of teacher inquiry to classroom learning is that engagement in inquiry helps students develop the skills necessary to be successful in the 21st century.

Another benefit of engaging students in inquiry emerges from the creative acts students engage in as a natural part of the inquiry process. These include activities such as "writing stories, newspapers, magazines, and speeches; creating websites and PowerPoint presentations; drawing artwork; performing plays; building models; painting murals; producing films; and designing posters, lab reports, and brochures" (Wolk, 2008, p. 121). Applying teacher inquiry to student learning means that in the act of creating something to show what was learned, students learn "to value and appreciate the thought and discipline required to produce excellence and to feel the pride that comes with making something with their own hands and minds" (Wolk, 2008, p. 121).

Finally, and perhaps most important, students who engage in inquiry are motivated to learn. Assignments that engage students in inquiry topics of their own choosing are intrinsically interesting to students. Students involved in inquiry often have to take an independent position in relation to a topic or issue. Rather than merely memorizing and repeating facts, students pose questions, collect information, analyze their findings, and then share their results. Other students may challenge their conclusions. Because the self-selected topics may sometimes be controversial (school dress codes, gangs, climate change, etc.), they provide a rich resource for teaching important skills such as distinguishing between fact and opinion, understanding statistical summaries, formulating persuasive arguments, and giving and receiving constructive feedback.

WHAT ARE THE CHALLENGES OF INSTITUTING STUDENT INQUIRY IN THE CLASSROOM?

Perhaps the biggest challenge associated with instituting student inquiry in the classroom is fear of giving up a teacher-directed, lecture-based, test-driven curriculum. According to Tony Wagner (2008), author of *The Global Achievement Gap*, "there is only one curriculum in American public schools today: test prep" (p. 71). Many teachers believe that the only way to ensure that students are prepared for high-stakes tests is to drill and practice for those tests. Teachers fear that abandoning traditional didactic instruction will mean that their students' performance on standardized tests will plummet. In fact, the opposite is true. Learning through inquiry is consistent with powerful instructional activity because engagement in inquiry makes learning *immediate, relevant, differentiated, self-directed, collaborative, active,* and *engaging.* In addition, inquiry helps students develop the skills necessary to be successful in the 21st century, including the specific skills necessary to acceptable performance on high-stakes tests.

Although teachers may worry about giving up the perceived control they have over the learning environment when teaching in a lecture-based, direct-instruction manner, their worries are unfounded. Over time, by using inquiry, teachers are better able to meet the learning needs of all students, without sacrificing test scores. According to Wolk (2008), teachers do not have to choose between students knowing important content to prepare them for a test and developing a healthy intellectual curiosity about their world through inquiry. Student engagement in inquiry helps teachers achieve both goals, and more.

In order to achieve these multiple goals simultaneously, teachers and administrators must know and understand standards and associated testing of those standards comprehensively. They need to appreciate that standards are friends of inquiry, rather than foes. A common misconception about inquiry is that it is a "free-for-all" learning experience—whatever the students want to learn is what they do—and that student interests take precedence above all (including curriculum standards). This misconception can be a huge challenge to instituting inquiry in the classroom and must be corrected immediately. Inquiry is not "discovery learning" and it is not about "letting students do whatever they want" (Wolk, 2008, p. 119). Additionally, inquiry does not mean *never* lecturing or *never* engaging the class in whole-class instruction. Rather, inquiry merely means that these are not the sole and dominant forms of pedagogy the teacher employs. Using inquiry, the teacher strikes a balance between giving students a voice in their own learning with regard to their interests and ideas and meeting explicit curricular objectives. The way to strike the balance between control and explicit curriculum objectives on the one hand and student interest and autonomy on the other is with a deep understanding of standards and the associated content knowledge students need to master. This understanding provides the teacher with the freedom to become a curriculum creator rather than a curriculum deliverer, and it restores creativity to the act of teaching. According to Wolk (2008),

> Students who learn through inquiry are immersed in content knowledge. Teachers make specific academic knowledge a fundamental part of an inquiry experience. Students may not be studying graphing out of a textbook, but they're learning that same content by graphing real data from a real survey they researched, created, and analyzed.
>
> State standards don't say, "Teach students geology from a textbook" or "Have kids learn about the American Revolution through a lecture." Standards list what kids should learn. They don't describe how they should learn. An advocate of inquiry-based teaching should not fear standards. On the contrary, the standards can support and justify teaching through inquiry. In addition, one long, well-planned integrative inquiry unit will satisfy dozens of learning standards. (p. 122)

In sum, the first and greatest challenge of instituting inquiry with students is for teachers and administrators to know the standards well enough that they can abandon overreliance on textbook learning with the full confidence they will be meeting all curricular objectives and standards through an inquiry approach to teaching.

Abandoning sole reliance on textbook learning leads to a related challenge many teachers face when engaging students in inquiry. A teacher who institutes inquiry as a form of pedagogy in his or her classroom by necessity must live with a certain amount of ambiguity. In the words of a teacher whose students conduct inquiry, "the process is messy." Teaching through inquiry means teachers must allow for a certain amount of spontaneity in instruction in order to respond to what students are asking and discovering. And, similar to the challenge of time discussed in the chapters on principal and teacher inquiry, allowing for spontaneity in instruction can lead to increased planning time for the teacher, as he or she shifts direction based on something that emerged in class on any given day.

Extended planning and replanning time must be incorporated into a teacher's schedule. A teacher shifts from *leading* the content and learning through lecture to *following the lead* of the students as they pose questions about content and engage in active investigations to gain insights into their own questions. A teacher shifts from *dispensing* knowledge to *facilitating* knowledge construction by creating the opportunity for students to interact with and explore content on their own and in collaboration with their classmates. A teacher shifts from being *in charge of every student's learning* to *empowering students to take charge of their own learning* with carefully guided scaffolding and support. Although making these shifts can be intimidating and time consuming, there is clear evidence that students' engagement in inquiry creates a powerful, healthy, and productive learning environment (Brickman, Gormally, Armstrong, & Hallar, 2009; Darling-Hammond et al., 2008; Luckie, Maleszewski, Loznak, & Krha, 2004).

A final challenge in promoting student inquiry lies in getting students to ask questions. Although young children appear to have an endless supply of questions, older students rarely ask questions. Instead, they expect the teacher to question them, usually with a predetermined answer in mind. This behavior is clearly a result of an educational system that reinforces rote memorization in tightly defined content areas, with little time or space for higher-order thinking. Students play a passive role; they take in information from a lecture or reading assignment and are expected to reproduce that information, usually on an objective test.

Teachers who want to promote an inquiry stance in their students have to overcome the students' learned tendency to see learning as a passive act (Edwards, 2004). In inquiry, students must grapple with a question or dilemma, using their previous knowledge and their reasoning ability to decide what they will study, how they will collect information, and how they will draw conclusions from the information. Students in inquiry classrooms are involved in their learning; they ask questions about why and how. Learning is fun and exciting.

How Can Teachers Introduce Student Inquiry Into the Curriculum?

As discussed in the previous section, engaging students in the process of inquiry is not a substitute for teaching any standards for student learning at the school, district, state, and/or national level. One way to introduce inquiry into the curriculum is to become intimately familiar with the standards, goals, and curriculum objectives for a given unit of study; reflect deeply on the ways those standards, goals, and curriculum objectives have been covered in the past; and assess whether engaging students in inquiry might be a viable and valuable alternative to past practices.

To be sure students' engagement in inquiry aligns with standards, those who advocate for teaching through inquiry suggest framing a unit with one or more questions called "essential questions" or "guiding questions" (see Bell, Smetana, & Binns, 2005; Ciardiello, 2003; Wilhelm, 2007).

> Judi Kur, a teacher we worked with at Radio Park Elementary School in State College, Pennsylvania, was uncomfortable with her teaching of a required first-grade science unit on dinosaurs. Judi had taught this unit for years, but upon reflection, she was troubled with the emphasis the unit seemed to place on "facts" and "cute activities," rather than engaging her young learners as scientists and allowing them to experience the process of inquiry first hand in a developmentally appropriate way. Judi decided to rethink the entire unit by engaging her first-grade learners with the following guiding question: "How do scientists know so much about dinosaurs?"

A second wonderful way that teachers can introduce student inquiry into the curriculum is to pair student inquiry with the teacher's own inquiry. In Judi Kur's case, as she was reworking the ways she traditionally taught the dinosaur unit to be inquiry based, she simultaneously utilized the process of teacher inquiry to understand how her newly developed inquiry-based unit was playing out in her classroom.

> Judi framed her own inquiry around engaging her students in inquiry, finding her first wondering in the tension that existed between the required teaching of this outdated unit on dinosaurs that focused on the acquisition of facts and a specific topic that was highly motivating for her primary age children. In Judi's words,

>> *I first thought about my inquiry project about the same time I began contemplating my upcoming responsibilities as the Chair of a unit entitled Prehistoric Life and Fossils. In my district, teachers are organized into teams that collaborate to teach four thematic, literature-based units each school year. As the Unit Chair, it was my responsibility to organize activities, orchestrate the sharing of books and materials among the teachers on my team, and lead the development of a culminating activity at the close of the unit.*
>>
>> *I had been dissatisfied with most of the science units in the primary curriculum since I began teaching first grade in 1996. I enjoy science and am fascinated with teaching science. However, to me science curriculum should focus on topics that children can experiment with, topics where the students can use the scientific process to ask and answer questions. This had not been my experience with the dinosaur unit. Yes, the children love the topic and they are motivated to learn, but I didn't feel that I was taking advantage of the children's and my enthusiasm. This unit as it was written didn't help me. In addition, a survey of the primary teachers in the district showed that most teachers thought the unit was extremely outdated. The science curriculum focuses on fossils, and the objectives can be covered in about a week,*

and to top it off, we were being told that we cannot use the word "theories" in our teaching of the unit, due to concerns expressed by parents that the dinosaur unit was teaching evolution and this was contrary to their religious beliefs.

Is it any wonder that when I last taught the dinosaur unit, the learning the children did was reading about other people's discoveries, not making their own? My students, as those mentioned by Craig Munsart in his book Investigating Science With Dinosaurs *(1993), "easily memorized names and dimensions of dinosaurs but learned little about the science that surrounds them." And yet I agreed with a statement that I read by Don Lessem in an article in the New York Times (1991):*

Dinosaurs are often a child's first introduction to science. As such, they could be the key to engendering a lifelong interest in all science.

And so, I wondered ... How can I take a science unit that is heavy on content and make it more science inquiry based? After reading the book Organizing Wonder: Making Inquiry Science Work in the Elementary School *(1998) by Jody Hall and talking with Carla Zembal-Saul, a professor in science education at the university, I embarked on developing lessons for this unit framed around the question, "How do scientists know so much about dinosaurs?" Once my lessons were developed and implemented, I pondered an additional research question: "What evidence exists that my newly developed inquiry-based lessons on dinosaurs help children develop the abilities advocated by the National Science Standards in the section that discusses science as inquiry?" (Kur, 2000)*

Judi Kur embedded her own inquiry-based learning within the engagement of her students in the process of inquiry, creating a beautifully intricate and intertwined web of teacher and student learning in her classroom, thus demonstrating teaching at its best.

More than merely engaging students in authentic inquiry investigations, we want to immerse them in a *culture* of inquiry. I can't reduce the essence of inquiry to a recipe. A culture of inquiry happens when teachers breathe inquiry as a part of their lives. . . . The best teachers I know aren't good just because of what they do in their classrooms for six hours a day; they're good teachers because of how they live their lives 24 hours a day. These teachers live a life filled with learning, thinking, reading, and debating. Because inquiry is an important part of their lives, inquiry becomes an essential part of their classroom. (Wolk, 2008, p. 119)

Inquiry became an essential part of Judi's classroom in ways that will be explored in Chapter 6.

WHAT ROLE DOES STUDENT INQUIRY PLAY IN THE DISTRICTWIDE PROFESSIONAL DEVELOPMENT PROGRAM?

One of the great benefits of job-embedded learning through inquiry is that it targets the enhancement of teacher quality and student achievement simultaneously. Teacher quality is enhanced through teacher learning. As teachers learn through engagement in inquiry, their learning is wrapped directly around the learning of their students in their classroom. This automatically makes students one essential piece of the districtwide professional development plan puzzle, but the student's role does not end there. Students can be engaged in the process of inquiry in the same ways the adults in the district continue their learning throughout their professional lifetimes. Learning becomes the way of being and the way of work for every person in the district—adults and children alike—making schools places of genuine wonder and critical inquiry.

WHERE CAN I LEARN MORE ABOUT STUDENT INQUIRY?

There is a plethora of articles and books that discuss student inquiry. To help you start exploring this powerful form of pedagogy with students, we have organized some of our favorite selections into two categories: general literature and subject-specific literature. For a wonderful overview of the benefits of engaging students as inquirers, we suggest you start with the article quoted often in this chapter by Steven Wolk, and continue with additional resources based on your interest and classroom context.

General Literature on Student Inquiry

- Wolk, S. (2008). School as inquiry. *Phi Delta Kappan, 90*(2), 115–122.
- Darling-Hammond, L., Barron, B., Pearson, P. D., Schoenfeld, A. H., Stage, E. K., Zimmerman, T. D. . . . Tilson, J. L. (2008). *Powerful learning: What we know about teaching for understanding.* San Francisco: Jossey-Bass.
- Edwards, C. H. (2004). *Teaching and learning in middle and secondary schools: Student empowerment through learning communities.* Upper Saddle River, NJ: Prentice Hall.

Subject-Specific Literature on Student Inquiry

Science

- Center for Science, Mathematics, and Engineering Education. (2000). *Inquiry and the National Science Standards: A guide for teaching and learning.* Washington, DC: National Academy Press.

- Edwards, C. H. (1997). Promoting student inquiry. *The Science Teacher,* *64*(7), 18–21.
- Brickman, P., Gormally, C., Armstrong, N., & Hallar, B. (2009). Effects of inquiry-based learning on students' science literacy skills and confidence. *International Journal for the Scholarship of Teaching and Learning,* 3(2). Retrieved from http://www.georgiasouthern.edu/ijsotl
- Luckie, D. B., Maleszewski, J. J., Loznak, S. D., & Krha, M. (2004). Infusion of collaborative inquiry throughout a biology curriculum increases student learning: a four-year study of "teams and streams." *Advances in Physiology Education,* *28*(4), 199–209.

Technology

- Callison, D. (1999). Key words, concepts and methods for information age instruction: A guide to teaching information literacy. *School Library Media Activities Monthly,* *15*(6), 38–42.

Mathematics

- Stonewater, J. K. (2005). Inquiry teaching and learning: The best math class study. *School Science and Mathematics, 105,* 36–47. Retrieved from http://findarticles.com/p/articles/mi_qa3667/is_200501/ai_n9467815/

Language and Literacy

- Wilhelm, J. D. (2007). *Engaging readers and writers with inquiry.* New York: Scholastic.
- Ciardiello, A. V. (2003). To wander and wonder: Pathways to literacy and inquiry through question finding. *Journal of Adolescent and Adult Literacy,* 228–239.

Social Studies

- Brickman, J. (2010). *Lesson ideas to enrich student inquiry into the Holocaust.* Scholastic.com. Retrieved from http://www2.scholastic.com/browse/lessonplan.jsp?id=395
- Levstik, L. S., & Barton, K. C. (2001). *Doing history: Investigating with children in elementary and middle schools.* Mahwah, NJ: Lawrence Erlbaum Associates.

REVIEW AND LOOKING AHEAD

In this chapter, we

1. defined student inquiry,

2. discussed benefits and challenges of instituting student inquiry in the classroom,

3. suggested ways teachers can introduce student inquiry into the curriculum,

4. reviewed the role student inquiry plays in the districtwide professional development program, and

5. suggested additional resources for learning more about student inquiry and the power of this pedagogical approach to teaching and learning.

In Chapter 6, we will illustrate the ways student inquiry can play out in elementary, middle, and high school contexts through the stories of teachers from across the country who engage students as inquirers: Judi and Marcia (State College, Pennsylvania), Randy and Wendy (Gainesville, Florida), and Jeanette and Julie (Madison, Wisconsin).

6

Student Inquiry in Practice

The Stories of Elementary, Middle, and High-School Teachers

When the work and understandings of teachers as researchers are followed by a concern with students as researchers, pedagogical possibilities abound. . . . Teachers will find a gold mine of instructional ideas that will not only challenge and expand their storehouse of pedagogical methods but will induce them to rethink their purposes as educators.

—Shirley Steinberg and Joe Kincheloe (1998, p. 19)

Inquiry can be a powerful way for students to learn. This chapter tells three stories that exemplify learning through inquiry in elementary, middle, and high schools. Each story reveals how engaging students in inquiry can be integrated seamlessly with subject area content standards. The third story also reveals how inquiry can be developed as a stand-alone elective for secondary students. We begin with a continuation of the Judi Kur dinosaur story from Chapter 5.

STORY 1: STUDENT INQUIRY IN ELEMENTARY SCHOOL

Judi and Marcia (State College, PA)

Recall from Chapter 5 that first-grade teacher Judi Kur was dissatisfied with a unit on dinosaurs, a unit Judi and many of her colleagues affectionately referred to as "prehistoric." Judi wondered, "How can I take a science unit that is heavy on content and make it more investigation based?" and "What evidence exists that my newly developed investigation-based lessons on dinosaurs help children meet the National Science Standards?"

> "How can I take a science unit that is heavy on content and make it more investigation based?"

To answer these questions, Judi reworked the unit on dinosaurs around one guiding inquiry question: "How do scientists know so much about dinosaurs?" To answer this question, she divided her class into paleontology teams. Each team received clues from a dig site about a "mystery dinosaur" and had to use the clues to discover the mystery dinosaur's identity.

After students received clues, they applied what they learned to their mystery dinosaur. For example, Judi's students experimented with the ratio between their own foot and leg length and their body height to determine how clues about their mystery dinosaur's foot size could help them determine its height.

As Judi was supporting her students in the inquiry process to discover the identity of their dinosaurs, she was simultaneously engaging in teacher inquiry to understand the ways her students were learning through investigation. Judi collected data by taking anecdotal notes, keeping a journal, looking at students' paleontology notebooks, taking pictures, and talking with other teachers. To analyze her data, she compared her data with the National Science Standards. Judi's inquiry into her students' learning showed clearly that her revised dinosaur unit was enabling her to meet the national standards.

For example, one National Science Standard asks, "Do students use data to construct reasonable explanations?" A student wrote in his notes:

> we discoverd that it is hard to see with nonstearyovishin because things look flat and starieovishin it looks 3-d because your eyes work togethr and meat eaters have starieovishin and plant eaters don't.

This was clear evidence that students were using data to construct reasonable explanations.

Another science standard asks, "Do students develop explanations using observations and what they know?" One group of students had received the drawing of a skull. They were asked, "What do you know about this dinosaur now?" Student responses included the following:

> We think it's a meateater because it has canines, and its eyes are close to the nostrils.

This was clear evidence that students were developing explanations using observations and what they know.

A third science standard asks, "Do students review and question each other's work?" Judi wrote the following in her journal:

> When they shared their skeletons and what they thought. . . . Other members asked questions and made comments like, "I don't think so, look the head is different." Or, "You must be right, look at the feet, they look like the ones you cut out." How exciting to hear them not only interested in their own dinosaur, but in other groups' as well.

Here was clear evidence that students were reviewing and questioning each other.

Once Judi's students had discovered the identity of their mystery dinosaur, they worked with a computer program, Kid Pix, and pictures Judi had taken to create a presentation describing the process of their learning and how they discovered the identity of their mystery dinosaur.

Judi's engagement of her young learners in this inquiry project was such a powerful and motivational learning experience for them that Judi's whole approach to teaching science was transformed. With evidence from her own research that she was meeting the National Science Standards using inquiry-based instruction, Judi set out to apply what she learned about teaching through inquiry to other units of study. The following year, Judi worked with a colleague, Marcia Heitzmann, to teach their students a unit on magnets using student inquiry. Judi and Marcia published their work focused on engaging students as inquirers in *Science and Children* (Kur & Heitzmann, 2008). In this article, Judi and Marcia explained their hopes and fears for teaching a required unit through inquiry:

> Though we agreed in principle with research that shows that inquiry-based teaching leads to positive attitudes toward science (Shymansky, Kyle, and Alport, 1983), we weren't sure if we could really teach about magnets in a meaningful way through inquiry. We were concerned that our first graders rarely posed wonderings as testable questions, and we worried about not being able to meet district content objectives regarding magnets. Our experience laid these concerns to rest.

By restructuring our lessons, using science talks, and listening carefully to our students, we were able to transform students' surprises and wonderings into testable questions and meet district learning objectives for magnets.

With this successful experience under our belts, we can approach inquiry teaching with more confidence. (p. 29)

Because their students were learning about sorting in math, Judi and Marcia kicked off their magnet unit with a sorting activity to pique student interest in magnetism. Students were paired and given a bin of materials that contained paper, plastic, wood, and metal. All bins contained different materials, but each contained a magnet and some objects that were attracted to magnets. Students were to develop a "rule" for sorting the materials in their bin. As students worked, Judi and Marcia circulated around the room asking questions and listening to student ideas. One pair of students tried sorting by heavy and light objects. The students explained that they had designed a test in which they balanced a Popsicle stick on a small block, placing each item in their bin on one side of the Popsicle stick. The students said, "If the stick goes down when we put it there, then we sort it as heavy. If it doesn't go down, we sort it as light!" By circulating and questioning students, Marcia and Judi were scaffolding their students to "think, test, and explain" like scientists.

This activity was followed by a science talk during which students shared their rules for sorting. As Judi and Marcia had planned and hoped, many students sorted by items that were attracted to magnets and those that were not. This talk led to the introduction of the magnet unit and generated great discussion and disagreements among the students as Judi and Marcia asked these questions:

- How could you tell something was attracted to a magnet?
- What items were attracted?
- What items were not attracted?
- What items in our classroom might be attracted?
- What items do you think would not be attracted?

There were disagreements, and some students expressed uncertainty about answers. Marcia and Judi asked whether the students wanted to learn more about magnets. The response was a resounding, enthusiastic first-grade chorus, "Yes!"

This first lesson set the tone for the entire unit and gave these first-grade learners the message that their questions mattered; they had voice in what they would study.

Setting the stage for the children to be in charge of their own learning, Judi and Marcia followed this introductory lesson with a free exploration of magnets. Students were instructed to circulate around the classroom, magnet in hand, and select three items they were sure would be attracted to a magnet, three items they were sure wouldn't be attracted to the magnet, and three items they were unsure about. As their students experimented, Marcia and Judi helped them turn their observations into "wonderings":

> When Charlie was surprised that the magnet was attracted to the metal table but not the metal chair, we helped him turn the statement into the wondering, *Are magnets attracted to all metals?* We helped him do this by first asking him why that surprised him. He said he thought it would stick because the table and chair are both metal, and magnets stick to metal. We stated, "But it wasn't attracted to the metal on the chair. What are you thinking now?" He said, "I don't think they stick to all metals." Similarly, when Jessica noticed that she could make a paper clip stick to a magnet through a book, we helped her turn that into the wondering, *Can magnets stick through things?* (p. 30)

Can magnets stick through things?

As student wonderings emerged, Judi and Marcia continued to create learning situations and investigatory lessons for their students, to help refine their wonderings and generate additional wonderings that would lead to the students deepening their understanding of physical science (Standard B of the National Science Education Content Standards for Grades K–4 focused on properties of objects and materials and magnetism) as well as ensure that students generated wonderings that aligned with each benchmark listed in their district's magnetism learning module. Figure 6.1 summarizes the wonderings Marcia and Judi's students generated and their alignment with the district's module content benchmarks.

Figure 6.1   Student Magnet Wonderings Aligned With District Benchmarks

Module Content	Student Wonderings
Magnets attract some objects.	What metals do magnets stick to?
Magnets attract objects through materials.	Can magnets work through things?
Like poles repel; unlike poles attract. All magnets have a north and south pole.	Do all magnets have sides that like and don't like each other?
The north pole of a magnet points to the magnetic north pole of the Earth.	Can we find the north pole with a magnet?
Magnets are useful to humans. There are many kinds of magnets. They must be handled with care.	Are some magnets stronger than others? Can we make other things into magnets? Can we break a magnetic field?

With a solid list of wonderings, Judi and Marcia abandoned their traditional approach to teaching science in which they would have provided the experimental set up and procedures for their students. Instead, Judi and Marcia presented one student wondering at a time, asking for ideas as to how they might go about answering the question. For example, when asked how they might answer the wondering, "Are some parts of a magnet stronger than others?" student ideas included "Make a chain of paper clips and use different parts of the magnet to see what part makes longer chains" and "Put paper clips at different distances from the magnet and see how far away different parts of the magnet could attract paper clips." Judi and Marcia drew upon the different ideas students had to provide multiple opportunities for investigations around a single concept. When engaged in these investigations and follow-up science talks in which the class came together to share and discuss what they had learned, students both clarified and deepened their understandings and also developed new wonderings, and the cycle of inquiry continued.

After many cycles through this process of wondering, investigation, science talk, and new wonderings, the teachers closed the unit by leading their class in constructing a list of their "learnings," insisting that each learning statement be supported by multiple examples of evidence (see Figure 6.2). This list became the foundation for the culminating activity, a science conference attended by parents, the principal, and some other teachers during which students worked in teams, chose a learning statement, and designed and performed a demonstration that provided evidence for their learning statement. Judi and Marcia reflect on their experiences:

> ". . . by using their questions, we empowered our students to become scientists."

We discovered that as we questioned and listened to our students, the wonderings we helped them develop led them to a deeper understanding of the content, and these wonderings naturally aligned with the module's content benchmarks and more . . . We also discovered that by using their questions, we empowered our students to become scientists.

They learned that their questions were important and that they were capable of answering them. As the unit progressed, students asked richer questions and provided more in-depth explanations. As a result of this unit, our students learned not only the content but also how to ask questions and how to talk to their peers—key processes of science—and they all developed a love for (or at least a keen interest in) science. (Kur & Heitzmann, 2008, p. 32)

Figure 6.2   Judi and Marcia's Student Learning Summary

What We Learned About Magnets	Our Evidence
Magnets are attracted to some metals.	The magnet stuck to one bell but not the other. The magnet stuck to one coin but not the other. The magnet stuck to one spoon but not the other.
Magnets work through wood, plastic, glass, water, and paper.	The paper clip stuck to the magnet through the plastic, glass, water, and paper.
Magnets are different strengths. Sizes or shapes don't matter.	The little round magnet held 200 paper clips, but the big horseshoe magnet only held 10 paper clips. The wand magnet held 150 paper clips, and the bar magnet held 5.
The ends of a bar magnet are strongest. The sides of the round magnet are strongest. The ends of the horseshoe magnet are strongest.	The ends held 10 paper clips, and the middle only held 5. The sides of the round magnet held 20 paper clips, the edge held only 8. The ends of the horseshoe magnet held 4 paperclips and the middle held none.
Magnetic things can be magnetized.	We could magnetize the scissors so that they would pick up the pins. We could magnetize the paper clips to pick up the pins.
The only thing that can break the magnetic field is another magnet.	Paper didn't make the paper clip fall. Wood didn't make the paper clip fall. Metal didn't make the paper clip fall. Plastic didn't make the paper clip fall. Another magnet made the paper clip fall.
All magnets have sides that attract and repel.	We could make all the magnets push or pull other magnets.

STORY 2: STUDENT INQUIRY IN MIDDLE SCHOOL

Randy and Wendy (Gainesville, FL)

After reading Tony Wagner's (2008) *The Global Achievement Gap: Why Even Our Best Schools Don't Teach the New Survival Skills Our Children Need—And What We Can Do About It,* Randy Hollinger, a seventh-grade life science teacher at P.K. Yonge Developmental Research School, became concerned that his middle schoolers were not learning the skills they would need to be successful in the 21st century. Randy set out to integrate technology into instruction in meaningful ways, teaching his students digital literacy while simultaneously engaging them in scientific inquiry to meet the objectives of his seventh-grade life science curriculum.

A self-described risk taker, but also "a teacher who was not proficient in much technology-wise other than e-mail and wikis," Randy set out to explore the question "How can I utilize technology as a tool in my teaching to help students both develop digital literacy skills and experience the process of scientific inquiry as it relates to the seventh-grade science curriculum?" First, Randy realized that he needed to deepen his own knowledge of technology and the ways it could be utilized to scaffold student learning. To achieve this goal, he connected with a teaching colleague, Wendy Drexler. Wendy taught high school in a nearby town and was knowledgeable about technology and the ways it could promote powerful learning opportunities for kids. The previous year, Wendy had experimented with her high school students, having them construct personal learning environments for the purpose of independent inquiry (Drexler, 2010b). *Personal learning environments* (PLEs) are defined as systems such as a desktop application or one or more web-based services that enable students to manage the content and process of their own learning as well as share what they have learned with others. PLEs integrate formal and informal learning experiences, social networks, and web services into personally managed computer space for each learner.

Based on her experiences facilitating students' construction and management of personal learning environments, Wendy was working to further develop this model of teaching she termed, "the networked student." (See Wendy's explanation of the networked student on YouTube at http://www.youtube.com/watch?v=XwM4ieFOotA.) Wendy agreed to help Randy become more familiar with useful technology as well as the ways he might help his students put this technology to work to engage in the process of inquiry (Drexler, 2010a). As Randy was becoming familiar with more technology tools, he also knew he needed to think deeply about his curriculum and the standards as he integrated technology and digital literacy into his science classroom.

Randy reviewed the state and national standards. In addition, he reviewed the International Society for Technology in Education National Technology Standards for Students. He summarized the relevant educational standards from these three organizations into a table to guide the development and implementation of his new technology-rich inquiry-based approach to teaching. Randy's table is available on the companion website to this book (Resource 1).

To launch his students into creating PLEs and the role they could play in inquiry-based science, Randy introduced them to the same technology tools he had learned from Wendy. All of his students were familiar with and comfortable utilizing e-mail, an essential tool for managing the PLE. However, they were less familiar with these other essential tools that Randy introduced:

- Evernote. A note-taking program that helps students collect and organize information by allowing them to clip small bits of text or pictures from different websites for later reference; the program keeps track of where the information came from so if utilized at a later date, students can reference the material appropriately.
- Glogster. A program that allows students to create a digital, online, multimedia poster with text, video, audio recording, and graphics integrated on one page.
- Google Docs. A web-based method to share and collaborate on the creation of word-processing and other types of documents.
- Blogging. An online journal that allows students to incorporate multimedia into the articulation of their learning and serves to make student reflections public, viewable, and sharable.
- Delicious. A social bookmarking tool that allows students to share, organize, search, and manage bookmarks of web resources related to their studies.

Once students learned these tools, Randy introduced Symbaloo, an electronic organizational tool his students could use to create a "hub" or "home base" for all the resources they used for their learning.

As Randy was teaching these tools, he told students that once they had mastered multiple networking tools that would enable them to take charge of their own learning, they would embark together on a collaborative whole-class investigation to explore the following wonderings:

> Which web tool is best for the learning we want to do?

- What are our interests and what do we want to learn more about from the seventh-grade science curriculum?
- Which web tool is best for the learning we want to do?
- Which web tool is best for presenting our learning to others?
- How might these web tools serve to connect us to each other as well as to other people who might help with our research?
- How do we practice digital responsibility?
- How do we know what we're finding on the web is factual information?

In order to answer each of these questions, Randy created learning situations and investigatory lesson experiences for his learners. For example, in order to gain some insights into the very first question, "What are our interests and what do we want to learn more about from the seventh-grade science curriculum?" Randy selected YouTube videos related to seventh-grade science content, such as "Beaver Lumberjacks," "Cockroach Infestation," "Underwater Creature Camouflage," and "Antlion Death Trap," asking students to watch the videos and complete related activities aligned with the standards summarized in his table. Rules for using YouTube in class were established and included accessing only videos directed by the teacher and disregarding (not reading) any comments. In addition, as students worked on their laptops independently, Randy was able to monitor their activity through LanSchool, a simple classroom management software that enables the teacher to synchronize his or her monitor with all student computer monitors and enables the teacher to control students' computers.

To answer the question "How do we know what we're finding on the web is factual information?" Randy had the class explore the Pacific Northwest Tree Octopus website (http://zapatopi.net/treeoctopus.html), asking the students to determine whether the creature was real just because it was found on the Internet. Students were to conduct additional research, taking and defending a position on whether this creature was real or not. As a follow up, students were asked to view the YouTube Video "Slip and Slide," in which a person flies through the air and lands in a small pool of water about 100 yards away. Randy queried, "Is this real?" and "How could it be scientifically tested?" Once students had gained insights into the initial inquiry questions, Randy turned the process of inquiry to focus on science content.

Students selected either a poisonous or venomous creature that they wished to learn more about. Students first worked to differentiate between poisonous and venomous creatures. In order to stimulate interest and help students decide on their creature of study, Randy sent them each on a web quest with a partner, to find the scariest real animal on earth, taking notes using Evernote and tagging all sites found on Delicious.

Once students selected a creature, they developed wonderings about their creature and set out to answer their wonderings using the tools and processes they had learned during the whole-class digital literacy inquiry conducted the prior week. For example, one child selected the deathstalker scorpion and developed the wonderings, "How did the deathstalker scorpion get its name?" "How deadly is the deathstalker scorpion?" and "Where is its stinger, how big is it, and how does it work?" Students collected "data" or information from the Internet to gain insights into their wonderings, keeping track of and organizing their learning using Evernote, creating documents differentiating between venomous and poisonous creatures using Google Docs, blogging about what they learned during each class when time was allocated to exploration, bookmarking and sharing pertinent sites with their classmates using Delicious, and communicating with a real scientist to get feedback on the accuracy of their research findings using e-mail and/or Skype. Finally, students analyzed their collected information and created a multimedia poster to share what they learned through their inquiry using Glogster (see Figure 6.3). After students shared their posters with each other, a new inquiry topic was introduced by Randy, and the cycle began anew.

Figure 6.3   Glogster Poster Example

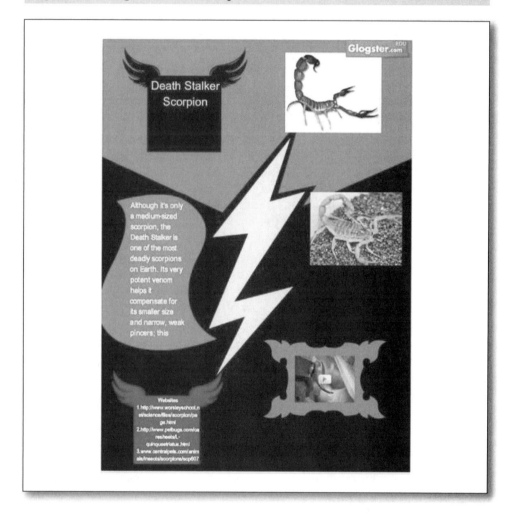

Randy's students were excited about science in ways that Randy had never experienced before in his 10 years of teaching. To experience the love and joy his students developed for technology and inquiry, visit http://www.youtube .com/watch?v=YEls3tq5wIY to see the PLE one of Randy's students created to engage in inquiry.

Randy's students were excited about science. . . .

Story 3: Student Inquiry in High School

Jeanette and Julie (Madison, WI)

Jeanette DeLoya and Julie Koenke are avid action researchers and have served as facilitators for other teachers learning to do inquiry. They work for Madison Metropolitan School District, an innovative district in Wisconsin that has a rich history of engaging teachers and administrators as inquirers (Caro-Bruce, Flessner, Klehr, & Zeichner, 2007). Jeanette and Julie shared not only a passion for coaching their district colleagues in action research, but also for raising student voice in their district. They wanted students to develop leadership skills to realize their capacity to effect change in the school district and the country in areas like social justice. Jeanette and Julie served as the faculty advisors of two different, related student groups in their districts. Judi advised Student Senate and Jeannette advised her district's Student Organization of the Minority Student Achievement Network, a national coalition of multiracial, suburban-urban school districts that are high-achieving school districts but have a significant achievement gap.

When discussing their advising responsibilities with each other, it occurred to Jeanette and Julie that their students could benefit from learning the same skills of inquiry that the teachers they worked with on action research across the district utilized as a venue for adult learning. Jeanette and Julie developed a .5-credit high school elective for student engagement in action research, called StAR (Student Action Research Course). Jeanette and Julie's overview of this high school elective and its organizational structure, as well as a sample lesson plan for the class's first meeting, are available on the companion website to this book (Resources 2 and 3).

The class met outside the regular high school day once a month. Students reflected on their development as leaders, learned the skills associated with enacting change through the process of action research, and received support and guidance as they engaged in their first action research project. Jeannette and Julie facilitated these monthly meetings, and students enrolled in this elective also selected an "advisor" from among faculty in the district or community members with related skills and interest in the student's research project, in much the same way as a doctoral student at a university works with an advisor to complete his or her dissertation. In addition to the monthly meetings, Jeanette and Julie also facilitated three weekly meetings a month called "Labs," where advisors and students could come for support through each step of the inquiry process.

Students were required to present the results of their research at a Student Leadership Summit and were also invited to participate in the annual Madison Wisconsin School District Teacher Action Research Forum. Student inquiry topics included the following:

- What is causing students to not meet the writing standard of their grade level? (Does it differ by "racial/ethnic" groups?) How do support programs cater to the writing skills of students?
- How have teacher-student relationships changed from elementary to middle to high school? How can what I learn be helpful to others?
- What is a student leader and how do teachers contribute to a student becoming a student leader?
- What can we do to ensure that all students are reading at the proper grade level at all times?
- In what ways can we use our knowledge and influence to encourage minority students to succeed in the classroom?
- Why do certain groups of students in the MMSD take more AP/ honors classes than other groups?
- How does test bias contribute to perceptions teachers have about student potential? How do we reduce the negative impact of test bias?

All student inquiries ended with recommendations for teachers and administrators in the district with many leading to change in practice and policy district-wide. Jeannette and Julie

> All student inquiries ended with recommendations for teachers and administrators in the district. . . .

were pleased to see that the value of action research for teacher learning in their district was readily transferrable to student learning. They had succeeded in raising student voice in district policy and providing practice in the skills necessary for students to become advocates for social justice.

QUESTIONS FOR DISCUSSION

Part III: For the Student

Part III of this text focused on applying the best of what we know about professional learning to the classroom. Reflect on Part III and apply what you've learned from the two chapters to your own context by answering the following questions:

1. Compare and contrast the three stories of students' engagement in inquiry in Chapter 6. In what ways are the stories similar? In what ways are they different?

2. Based on the similarities among the three stories articulated in your answer to the first question, develop a list of what you believe to be core features of effective student inquiry. Which of these features do you believe to be most essential to unleash the power engagement in inquiry holds for student learning?

3. Review the differences between the three stories articulated in your answer to the first question and discuss how each of the differences were related to the context in which the teacher worked (elementary, middle, high school). What ways could engagement in student inquiry be adapted for different contexts in your district (grade level and subject areas)?

4. How might you introduce student engagement in inquiry as a pedagogical tool to teachers in your district?

5. What do you feel would be the greatest benefit to engaging students in inquiry in your school or district?

6. What do you feel would be the greatest challenge to engaging student in inquiry in your school or district? How might these challenges be addressed?

7. How will you start the process of integrating inquiry into your classroom or school?

- What curriculum will you begin with?
- Who are your allies in this work for support?
- Where are you allowing for student voice?

PART IV

The Coach's Role

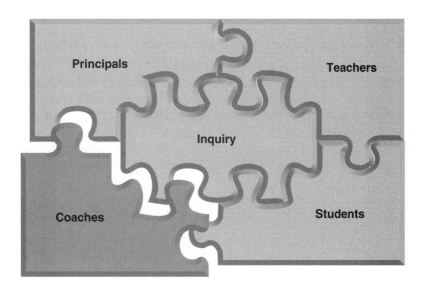

7

The Importance of Coaching

Coaches support teachers as they work together to grapple with problems of practice and to make smarter, collaborative decisions that are enriched by the shared practice of the entire community. When coaches choose roles and allocate their time and services to those that have the greatest potential for impacting teaching and student learning, the value of coaching and coaches will be unquestioned, even when budgets are tight and other competing priorities emerge.

—Killion (2009, pp. 27–28)

The opening quote to this chapter underscores the important role of coaching in building a districtwide, systemic, powerful professional development program. Although the concepts we have discussed so far in this book hold tremendous potential for improving the teaching and learning that occurs in schools, the quality of the professional development experience, and therefore the success inquiry holds for unleashing teacher quality and improving student achievement across a district, is directly related to the quality of the coaching received by educators engaged in this work. Effective coaching is the lynchpin upon which rests the success of the work we have described in this book.

The world of athletics provides a fine referent for understanding the importance of coaching. For example, golfer Tiger Woods, arguably one of the best athletes the world has seen, continually works with a swing coach and did so even at the height of his performance on the PGA tour. Coaches help athletes (even the most talented players) continually grow, develop, and adjust to the conditions under which a sport is played, thereby raising the quality of performance. In a similar fashion to athletics, coaches in the field of education can "raise the quality of the teaching and learning in every classroom in the school by building a culture in which

- teaching is public and itself the focus of study among professionals;
- planning for instruction is thorough and collaborative and digs deeply into the content; and
- conversations and questions about improving student results among teachers are constant, evidence-based, and nondefensive" (Saphier & West, 2009, p. 46).

Making teaching public and the focus of professional study, collaborative planning, and participation in deep, rich, meaningful, data-based conversations about teaching and learning are all essential to the work we have described in Parts I, II, and III of this book. Yet, these acts do not happen magically. Someone (or perhaps, more accurately, several someones) has to create the conditions that ensure that all professional educators in a district are able to continually learn and improve their practice. Although grammatically incorrect, the addition of the "s" to the word "someone" is important to highlight an underlying premise of our view of coaching in relationship to inquiry and job-embedded learning: *Everyone needs a coach and everyone can be a coach, but effective coaches are not born; they are made with careful, systematic, and intentional attention by a district to cultivating coaching skills systemwide.* Hence, this chapter explores the role of coaching in depth, beginning with an expanded definition of the ways many districts have conceptualized the role of coach to date.

WHAT IS A COACH?

We add to the traditional notion of coach and coaching by differentiating between a formal and defined coaching role held by an individual and a system in which all members of the district take on some responsibility for coaching. A *formal coach* is a support person (such as the central office professional development specialist, a reading coach, math coach, or other instructional coach) whose primary job responsibility is to focus on the professional learning of all adults across a district. In their book *Taking the Lead: New Roles for Teacher Leaders and School-Based Coaching,* Joellen Killion and Cindy Harrison (2006) describe 10 different roles for coaches in their work, noting that some coaches serve in all 10 roles while others only serve in a few and focus their energies on the roles that have the greatest potential to improve teaching and student learning. The 10 roles are data coach, resource provider, mentor, curriculum specialist, instructional specialist, classroom supporter, learning facilitator, school leader, catalyst for change, and learner. District personnel who are formally in a coaching role are essential to the work described in this book, and they weave job-embedded learning through inquiry into all the roles they play.

Given that everyone needs a coach to help shape powerful job-embedded learning experiences, there is an inevitable shortage of formal coaches. It would be impossible for even the wealthiest district in the nation to provide a formal coach for every educator in the district and give them a reasonable enough workload that they could spend quality time with their coachees, keep up with the latest research about best practices that might inform student learning in the district, and study their own coaching practice with other coaches in the district to lead, by example, in what they are asking their coachees to do. We suggest that although it is critical to have some resources dedicated to formal coaches whose primary job responsibility is a laser-like focus on the cultivation of adult learning, given the importance of coaching, districts must supplement formal coaches with informal coaches.

An *informal coach* is a district professional (such as a principal, assistant principal, or teacher) whose primary job is not focused on coaching, but who adopts the responsibility for supporting and sometimes leading job-embedded learning with his or her colleagues. For example, the fifth-grade team leader in an elementary school might reconceptualize the way he runs his grade-level meetings each Wednesday afternoon from focusing on logistical issues and paperwork to engaging all the fifth-grade teachers in a collaborative inquiry that emerges from a deep look at fifth graders' work schoolwide. A principal might reconceptualize the way she runs her leadership team meetings, positioning all members of the team as co-inquirers into a schoolwide issue. A department chair in a high school might reconceptualize weekly department meetings so that twice a month faculty bring student work and dilemmas to share with the group, and each member of the group engages in an inquiry focused on a particular struggling learner in the classroom. In each of these instances, the fifth-grade teacher, the principal, and the high school department chair take on the informal coaching role.

There exist several advantages to schools and districts that augment their formal coaching staff with informal coaches (teachers and administrators) to help with the task of coaching job-embedded professional learning. First and foremost, this informal coach is perceived as a peer—certainly as someone who is a member of the staff with the same commitment to student learning as all other staff members. Second, the informal coach has a built-in hook, in that he or she can pose a question in relation to his or her own practice: "I have noticed _____ in my classroom. Have you ever observed something similar?" This is an excellent way to guide teachers into a study of a specific educational issue, strategy, or dilemma. Third, the informal coach can be available for short, targeted conversations, for example early in the morning or while escorting a group of students across the campus, whereas those who occupy formal coaching roles often have to divide their energies between two or more schools, due to budget cuts in a district, and may not be readily available. Finally, teachers know that the informal coach has the same time constraints and responsibilities that they do and therefore can appreciate the unique features of their situation or classroom.

Just as there are some unique advantages to being an informal coach, there are some unique advantages to being a formal coach as well. Perhaps most important, because a formal coach's primary responsibility is to focus on adult learning, his or her energies don't need to be divided between fostering the learning of his or her students and the learning of his or her colleagues. Further, formal coaches can often work with a greater number of adult learners than can informal coaches, for a longer time. Additionally, formal coaches have more freedom and flexibility during school hours to go in and out of classrooms, helping teachers immediately and even collecting data for teachers. Whether serving in a formal or informal capacity, coaches provide many benefits for all educators when they facilitate job-embedded learning.

WHAT ARE THE BENEFITS OF PROVIDING COACHES TO FACILITATE JOB-EMBEDDED LEARNING?

We believe Joellen Killion, Director of Special Projects for Learning Forward and expert on professional development, teacher leadership, and coaching, has articulated two of the most salient benefits of providing coaches to facilitate job-embedded learning. First, according to Killion (2009), during coaching, "every school community engages in ongoing, ruthless analysis of data and continuous cycles of improvement that allow its members to measure results in a matter of weeks, not months or years" (p. 27). Hence, coaching speeds up a school's and district's ability to diagnose areas that need attention and provide attention to those areas in systematic and informed ways. Whether designated formally by title as "Coach" or serving as coach in an informal capacity, a coach's responsibility is to focus his or her gaze directly on creating the conditions that are ripe for adult members of the district to continually learn and improve. By having a designated responsibility to focus on adult learning, coaches enable schools and districts to continuously evolve and become better and better at meeting the needs of all teachers, all administrators, and most important, all students.

According to Killion (2009), a second benefit of providing coaches for teachers is that "no teacher ever faces an instructional challenge alone" (p. 27). We add a corollary to this important benefit: No principal ever faces an administrative challenge alone. As previously discussed in Chapters 1 and 3, teaching and being an administrator is lonely work, historically plagued, for the most part, by isolation. Coaches take teachers and principals out of isolation and into a relationship that provides support as well as pressure to learn, grow, change, and evolve as an educator in response to student needs.

Support and pressure are equally important in the coaching relationship. First, providing support is an essential component of coaching and should not be taken for granted. Inquiring into one's professional practice through job-embedded professional development is intense work. Everyone needs affirmation that his or her work as an adult learner is both valued and valuable.

Yet, support without pressure risks teachers and administrators feeling good about their practice without looking at that practice in new and different ways and making improvements in practice that will enhance teaching and learning. Having coaches who provide support without pressure could ultimately result in a district going through the motions of inquiry-oriented professional learning communities without rich, deep growth and development of learning community group members. All educators in the district may be happy and feel good about themselves, but they won't learn and change as a result of their job-embedded professional development work. A district's inquiry work might run smoothly and look good from the outside but appear shallow and hollow when looked at from the inside. This is one reason coaching is so crucial to the processes we have described in this book. Outstanding coaches know that providing some pressure is a critical part of the teacher and administrator professional development equation: Pressure + Support = Educator Learning and Change.

Sometimes coaches can exert pressure just by being willing to create some discomfort, and because creating discomfort is something that most educators are uncomfortable doing, it's important to have someone(s) purposely designated to that role.

> Coaching can move good teachers to become great teachers. It provides the strongest return on the investment of teaching. Coaches may cause discomfort at times. However, great coaches create environments where the coachee is comfortable with discomfort. Discomfort is key to growth and change. When good teachers become uncomfortable, that discomfort gives them impetus to improve, to wake up and get out of their box; it stimulates positive change. (Barkley, 2005, p. 21)

WHAT ARE THE CHALLENGES OF COACHING JOB-EMBEDDED LEARNING?

The first challenge of coaching job-embedded learning is finding just the right balance between pressure and support, comfort and discomfort. In general, it is much easier for a coach to provide support and become a cheerleader and advocate for colleagues, rather than exert pressure on the teacher or administrator to delve deeper into his or her thinking and teaching. "Pushing harder" is probably one of the most difficult aspects of being a coach. Coaches are sometimes afraid that pushing harder could lead to conflict, or worse yet, an educator retreating from job-embedded professional learning altogether, or the coach may be afraid that he or she will not be "liked" by colleagues. Because of this tension, it is not uncommon for some coaches to focus their energies almost exclusively on support, finding it difficult to perfectly balance the teacher and administrator professional development equation introduced in the previous section: Pressure + Support = Educator Learning and Change. The National School Reform Faculty offers a great protocol titled "Zones of Comfort, Risk, and Danger: Constructing Your Zone Map" that helps coaches and coachees openly discuss the tensions between pressure and support and their important relationship to adult learning.

A second challenge of coaching job-embedded learning is navigating the tensions that can exist between coaching and evaluation. First and foremost, it is important that the relationship between coach and administrator is clearly articulated. In a keynote speech at a Coaching Academy, Kathy Christensen, 2009 Florida Reading Coach of the Year, shared an important nugget of information about her formal coaching role: "Coaches are not administrators. Teachers need to view us as fellow teachers, which is exactly what we are. I would never go to my principal and report on a teacher and my teachers know this" (Christensen, 2009). Yet, at the same time they are separating themselves from administration, coaches need to cultivate strong relationships with them as well. The cultivation of a strong working relationship is essential because coach and principal are often the only two people who have interaction directly with *all* the teachers in the building and share a focus on improving teaching and learning schoolwide. Building this relationship becomes challenging when the coach reports to the principal, a common practice in many districts. Rather than report to the building principal, coaches should report to a district curriculum director or other similar district-level administrator.

> When coaches report to the district, the district can also specify what coaches cannot do. For example, principals often want assistance and are generally short staffed. When the role of the coach is evolving in a district, and when the coach reports to the principal, the principal has a great deal of latitude in how to employ the coach. In many instances, coaches can be found doing lunch or bus duty, working with only the most unskilled teachers, and doing administrative tasks, and they are often given virtually no time to plan with teachers and prepare for working with teachers. Often, principals are unclear how to best use a coach's services and end

up using this precious and expensive resource in ways that don't yield much gain. Sometimes, principals need assistance as instructional leaders in determining what effective instruction and evidence of significant learning in a particular content area (for example, mathematics) might entail. Most principals will probably find it easier to seek that help from educators who don't report directly to them, another reason why coaches should report to the district. (Saphier & West, 2009, p. 50)

The ever-present tensions between coaching and evaluation can play out in a second way that presents a challenge for informal coaching. In some schools where we have worked, a principal or assistant principal takes on the role of an informal coach and facilitates a group of faculty through a collective or individual inquiry. In these schools, there is potential for the coach role to conflict with the role of teacher evaluator. Teachers feel uncomfortable sharing certain dilemmas or problems with the principal who ultimately evaluates their performance. At larger schools where there is a principal and at least one assistant principal, these two can divide the roles systematically between them. One of them coaches inquiry while the other conducts annual performance appraisals for a group of teachers. If the administrative team establishes a process in which the administrator is either a coach or an evaluator, but never both, teachers may feel more comfortable sharing their struggles and dilemmas, and the professional learning culture of the school is enhanced. In smaller schools, where there is only a principal, the role of informal coach is best delegated to a teacher leader. In sum, a significant challenge of coaching is the separation of coaching and evaluation. By being both cognizant of and sensitive to teachers who worry about the potential repercussions associated with intermingling coaching and evaluation, both formal and informal coaches (even if coach and administrator are the same person) can be sure to keep these two processes distinct from one another.

Of course, a final challenge to coaching job-embedded professional development is finding and making the time to cultivate the coaching skills of all coaches—both formal and informal—throughout a district. Remember that good coaches are not born; they are made with careful, systematic, and intentional attention by a district to cultivating coaching skills systemwide. This won't happen by chance or magic; it must be built into a district's plan.

How Can a District Develop Coaches in and Across Schools?

One key action a district can take to develop coaches is to create the time and space for all coaches (formal and informal) to meet regularly to cultivate and deepen their skills as coaches.

> District leadership can provide time and resources for coaches to become a high-powered team with one another, sharing a common vision and mutual purpose. . . . What we've done in some larger districts is to form a team of all the coaches from the different geographic zones, sometimes in just one content area and sometimes across content areas. The coaching team then works together to strengthen the skills of all coaches, to build coherent images of effective instruction, and to collaboratively determine what constitutes evidence of student learning. (Saphier & West, 2009, p. 49)

Additionally, districts can utilize some of the suggestions in Chapter 3 for creative uses of time and money, to provide incentive and support for those who don't serve in a formal coaching role to take on this responsibility informally.

Districtwide coaching meetings create a space for formal and informal coaches to learn about important topics such as the inquiry process and utilizing protocols to structure adult conversation. To facilitate this learning, the district's professional development director or other members of the central office PD team often structure districtwide coach meetings. In addition, districts may tap into many outstanding national organizations, such as the National School Reform Faculty, School Reform Initiative, and Coalition of Essential Schools, and send coach representatives to training offered by these groups. In turn, these representatives return to the district and share what they learned with all district coaches.

WHAT ROLE DO COACHES PLAY IN THE DISTRICTWIDE PROFESSIONAL DEVELOPMENT PROGRAM?

Creating a districtwide professional development plan grounded in job-embedded learning and inquiry means that many different configurations of people are exploring and deepening their understanding of a variety of issues associated with the learning of all students across a district simultaneously. There is important work to be done to organize and coordinate the learning of all adult members of a district when their learning is allowed to emerge from and focus intently on the learning needs of the students they serve. Coaches play that important organizing and coordination role. Coaches provide both pressure and support for meaningful adult learning to unfold across the district, which inevitably leads to enhanced student achievement.

WHERE CAN I LEARN MORE ABOUT COACHING?

There are many excellent resources available that explore both the importance of and the intricacies inherent in coaching.

- Dana, N. F., & Yendol-Hoppey, D. (2008). *The reflective educator's guide to professional development: Coaching inquiry-oriented learning communities.* Thousand Oaks, CA: Corwin. This book is written directly to coaches, with chapters devoted to tips and processes for taking coachees through each critical juncture in the inquiry process: developing a wondering, developing a plan for inquiry, analyzing data, and sharing inquiry with others. This book also contains a chapter focused on explicating the 10 essential elements of healthy learning communities.

- Killion, J., & Harrison, C. (2006). *Taking the lead: New roles for teachers and school-based coaches.* Oxford, OH: National Staff Development Council. This book provides an extensive overview of coaching and is divided into two parts. Part One is titled "Describing the Roles," with one chapter on each of the 10 roles for coaches mentioned in this chapter: resource provider, data coach, curriculum specialist, instructional specialist, classroom supporter, mentor, learning facilitator, school leader, catalyst for change, and learner. Part Two is titled "Implementing and Sustaining the School-Based Coach Program," with one chapter devoted to each of the following topics: selecting coaches, district support, school support, partnership agreements, day-to-day work, evaluation, troubleshooting, and possibilities and pitfalls.

- Knight, J. (2007). *Instructional coaching: A partnership approach to improving instruction.* Thousand Oaks, CA: Corwin. This is a "how to" text for coaches; chapters cover the essential skills of coaching, discuss principles of effective coaching, review appropriate communication strategies for coaches to use with teachers, and lay out a vision of coaches as change agents in a district. Each chapter includes first-person stories from high-performing instructional coaches; a concise, clear summary of major points at the end of the chapter; and a list of suggested resources relevant to each chapter topic. This book is designed to be a resource for practicing coaches as well as educators who supervise coaching programs.

- Sweeney, D. (2010). *Student-centered coaching: A guide for K–8 coaches and principals* Thousand Oaks, CA: Corwin. With the express goal of increased student achievement, this book focuses coaching on specific goals for student learning, rather than on changing or fixing teachers. Many examples of coaches who support literacy, mathematics, science, and humanities as well as principals who are leading coaching in their schools are explored. Highlighting the importance of the coach-principal relationship discussed in this chapter, this book contains a series of tools that are designed to foster dialogue, problem solving, and collaborative planning between a principal and coach so they can work together to design and implement the student-centered coaching model. The book is organized into three sections, with Section One focusing on defining student-centered coaching and exploring key factors for establishing coaching efforts driven by student learning, Section Two exploring the role of data and student evidence in relationship to coaching, and Section Three explicating a variety of practices that underlie a student-centered coaching effort. Practices include how to engage adult learners while taking into account such factors as career stage, gender, and generation, and how districts can develop a system of support for coaches.

REVIEW AND LOOKING AHEAD

In this chapter, we

1. defined coach,

2. discussed the benefits and challenges of coaching job-embedded learning,

3. suggested ways to develop coaches across a district,

4. reviewed the role coaches play in the districtwide professional development program, and

5. suggested additional resources for learning more about coaching.

In Chapter 8, the ways a district might develop a cadre of coaches over time are illustrated by the story of Lauren, a newly appointed director of professional development for a large, urban district.

8

Developing a Districtwide Cadre of Coaches

The Story of Lauren, Professional Development Director

To invest in coaching, an expensive intervention, without the foresight to have someone working closely with coaches may be shortsighted on the district's part. One way that districts can support coaches is by identifying a coach "champion." The coach champion may be someone with other responsibilities such as a director of curriculum or professional development . . . The coach champion is the guardian of the coaching program to ensure that teachers and students receive the maximum benefit from coaches' work.

—Killion and Harrison (2006, pp. 111–112)

Lauren had just been appointed head of professional development of a large urban school district. For the past seven years, she had been an elementary principal, and she was excited about taking on this new challenge while simultaneously completing her doctorate in education. Through her doctoral studies she had become interested in the power of teacher inquiry to improve teaching and learning and had enjoyed analyzing the steps her district had been taking in a subset of the district's schools over the past few years, as administrators tinkered with job-embedded learning through inquiry. One reason she was looking forward to this new position was that her superintendent had made it clear to her when she interviewed that he wished to see a transformation in professional development over the next several years, moving away from what the superintendent referred to as "One Shot Wonders," where teachers would come together for the day and be talked at by an "expert" on the latest topic. Rather, seeing the powerful learning experiences some of the district's teachers had experienced through engaging in inquiry, Lauren's superintendent envisioned the district moving toward job-embedded learning as advocated by the national organization Learning Forward. In part, Lauren had been chosen because of her passion for and understanding of job-embedded learning.

Lauren recalled the conversation she had with her superintendent when she was hired for the position. When asked, "What do you think is the most important thing we need to do in our district to spread the power of job-embedded learning through inquiry?" Lauren replied, "The director of professional development can't do it all alone. One of the most crucial ingredients of a successful districtwide professional development plan is a cadre of skilled coaches who can help teachers and principals through each of the critical junctures of the inquiry process. Teachers know that powerful learning experiences for their students don't happen by chance; those experiences are carefully and deliberately scaffolded in a thoughtful, intentional way. Just as powerful learning doesn't happen for children on its own, neither can we expect it to happen for teachers on its own. All educators in our district need inquiry coaches if we truly want everyone to become the best they can be through job-embedded professional development.

The first thing I will do as director of professional development is recruit folks from across the district who are interested in coaching job-embedded learning. This will include the people we already have in the formal role of coaches, such as our reading and math coaches, but it will also include administrators and teachers who want to learn more about scaffolding their colleagues' professional learning as well as their own and who can serve as informal inquiry coaches. If everyone in our district needs a coach, we can't rely solely on the folks we have in formal coaching positions. We'll need to help administrators and teachers see that coaching can be a rewarding component of their jobs as well."

As the new director of professional development, one of Lauren's first tasks was to establish the structures necessary to support districtwide inquiry. She set up a district inquiry website accessible to all district employees. On this website her staff could post meeting agendas, published resources relevant to inquiry, compilations of feedback from inquiry meetings, individual teachers' inquiry write-ups, and information relevant to earning professional development credit through inquiry.

Next, Lauren began planning what she referred to as the district's first "Coaching Series": four meetings over the next year for those interested in exploring the role of coach in relationship to job-embedded learning through inquiry. She recruited one coach from each of the 45 schools in her district to join her in this exploration. Some of the people who signed up with Lauren for this Coaching Series were administrators, some were teachers interested in leading professional learning, and some were district employees already in the role of coach who wished to learn more about how they could weave the coaching of inquiry into their current positions.

To plan these four sessions, Lauren worked with a team of professional developers from her department as well as some of the people in the district who had coached inquiry in the past. Because finding time to pull together educators from across the district is always tricky and time is always precious, the planning team considered carefully the best timing and length for their meetings. In order to lay a solid foundation for the development of coaches across the district, they used a full day for the first coaching session. This meeting provided an orientation to job-embedded learning through inquiry and helped people interested in coaching understand some of the finer details of coaching inquiry. The first meeting took place in August during the pre-planning week before the start of the academic year. After this meeting, Lauren and the district PD team decided to hold the next two meetings after school from 3:00 to 5:00 and to schedule them around the times the coaches would be beginning to help their coachees develop plans to collect data for their inquiries (October) and analyze the data they collected (January). Knowing that publicly sharing the learning that had taken place through inquiry was of critical importance for both the inquirers and every other educator in the district, Lauren also planned a districtwide inquiry showcase to take place near the end of the school year. This would give the educators who engaged in inquiry that school year a benchmark to pace the development of their inquiry as well as hold them accountable for their learning through the process. Finally, Lauren knew both from her experiences and from her reading of scholars such as Andy Hargreaves and Michael Fullan that organizational change is slow. The shift from a system dominated by traditional models of professional development to a system facilitating job-embedded learning through inquiry would take longer than one year. Therefore, it would be imperative to assess the effectiveness of the first year of the efforts to spread inquiry districtwide. The last meeting in the coaching series was planned for May, to do just that. Lauren and the planning team constructed a calendar of their four-meeting Coaching Series to share with all the attendees at the first session in August. This calendar, easily adaptable to any context, is available on the companion website to this book (Resource 4).

August Meeting

Introductions and Inspiration

To kick off the coaching year, Lauren wished to begin with an introductory activity that would simultaneously help these educators from different schools get to know one another, begin a discussion of the process of inquiry, and model an important tool for any coaching practice: creating the space for educators to talk with one another in systematic and intentional ways to construct their own knowledge. With this is mind, Lauren selected a National School Reform Faculty protocol called "Block Party" (http://nsrfharmony.org/protocol/doc/block_party.pdf) to facilitate the start of her first coaches meeting.

Block Party Protocol

When coaches entered the room that morning, each individual received one of 12 different quotes about inquiry printed on a half sheet of paper, along with the agenda and other materials for the day (see Figure 8.1). Lauren welcomed the group and explained the opening activity by directing the participants to find the quote they received in their materials packet, read the quote, flip the quote over, and jot down a sentence or two that captured what that quote meant to them. Next, each person found someone they didn't know who did not have the same quote. Once everyone had a partner, Lauren told the group that they should introduce themselves to each other and then each take one minute to share their quote and what it meant to them.

After two minutes, Lauren got everyone's attention and said, "OK, great job sharing everyone. Next, you are to find another partner whom you don't know who has a different quote from both you and your current partner. Then, the sharing process will begin again."

After everyone had found a second partner and shared, Lauren repeated the sequence one more time and then asked everyone to return to their seats. She debriefed the experience by asking the whole group to share some of their reactions to the quotes. One high school principal said, "I like the notion of teachers owning their professional learning. Although I know I have problems with giving up control, it is clear to me that I cannot do everything in my huge high

> "I get tired of teachers saying, 'Just tell me what to do and I'll do it.'"

Figure 8.1   Block Party Inquiry Quotes

Teacher inquiry is a vehicle that can be used by teachers to untangle some of the complexity that occurs in the profession, raise teachers' voices in discussions of educational reform, and ultimately transform assumptions about the teaching profession itself.	Given today's political context, in which much of the decision making and discussion regarding teachers occurs outside the classroom (Cochran-Smith & Lytle, 2006; Darling-Hammond, 1994), the time seems ripe to create a movement where teachers are armed with the tools of inquiry and committed to educational change.
While both the process-product and qualitative research paradigms have generated valuable insights into the teaching and learning process, they have not included the voices of the people closest to the children— classroom teachers. Hence, a third research tradition emerges highlighting the role classroom teachers play as knowledge generators. This tradition is often referred to as "teacher research," "teacher inquiry," "classroom research," or "action research."	In general, the teacher inquiry movement focuses on the concerns of teachers (not outside researchers) and engages teachers in the design, data collection, and interpretation of data around their question. Termed "action research" by Carr and Kemmis (1986), this approach to educational research has many benefits: (1) theories and knowledge are generated from research grounded in the realities of educational practice; (2) teachers become collaborators in educational research by investigating their own problems; and (3) teachers play a part in the research process, which makes them more likely to facilitate change based on the knowledge they create.
Very simply put, inquiry is a way for me to continue growing as a teacher. Before I became involved in inquiry, I'd gotten to the point where I'd go to an inservice and shut off my brain. Most of the teachers I know have been at the same place. If you have been around at all you know that most inservices are the same cheese—just repackaged. Inquiry lets me choose my own growth and gives me tools to validate or jettison my ideas.	You know that nagging that wakes you in the early hours, then reemerges during your morning preparation time so you cannot remember whether you already applied the deodorant, later on the drive to school pushing out of mind those important tasks you needed to accomplish prior to the first bell, and again as the students are entering your class and sharing all the important things happening in their lives? Well, teacher inquiry is the formal stating of that nagging, developing a plan of action to do something about it, putting the plan into action, collecting data, analyzing the collected works, making meaning of your collection, sharing your findings, then repeating the cycle with the new nagging(s) that sprouted up.
Teacher inquiry is not something I do; it is more a part of the way I think. Inquiry involves exciting and meaningful discussions with colleagues about the passions we embrace in our profession. It has become the gratifying response to formalizing the questions that enter my mind as I teach. It is a learning process that keeps me passionate about teaching.	Teacher inquiry differs from traditional professional development for teachers, which has typically focused on the knowledge of an outside "expert" being shared with a group of teachers. This traditional model of professional growth, usually delivered as a part of traditional professional development, may appear to be an efficient method of disseminating information, but often it does not result in real and meaningful change in the classroom.

This movement toward a new model of professional growth based on inquiry into one's own practice can be powerfully developed, by school districts and building administrators, as a form of professional development. By participating in teacher inquiry, the teacher develops a sense of ownership in the knowledge constructed, and this sense of ownership contributes to the possibilities for real change to take place in the classroom.	By cultivating an inquiry stance toward teaching, teachers play a critical role in enhancing their own professional growth and ultimately the experience of schooling for children. Thus, an inquiry stance is synonymous with professional growth and provides a nontraditional approach to professional development that can lead to meaningful change for children.
Action research is a wonderful tool teachers can use to differentiate instruction, ultimately making schools a better place for all students, regardless of their interests, abilities, background, and learning styles.	By embracing an inquiry approach, teachers expand their idea of what data is and how using data can inform their teaching and enhance student learning. The inquiry stance embraced by teacher researchers supports both data-driven decision making and progress monitoring.

school. And frankly I get tired of teachers saying, 'Just tell me what to do and I'll do it.' I'm wondering how I can promote inquiry as a way for teachers to take charge of and responsibility for solving some of their own problems." An elementary reading coach chimed in, "The part I liked was where it said that inquiry is not something I do but rather it is part of how I think about my profession. I agree that we teachers need to assume responsibility for resolving dilemmas we encounter in our classrooms, but I don't know where to start."

To conclude, Lauren asked everyone to think about how they might use the block party protocol in their own contexts, and she used their discussion about the protocol as a segue into sharing the day's agenda and goals. As they looked at the agenda together, Lauren noted that the group would use the day to explore the following questions together: What exactly is inquiry anyway? What does it mean to coach inquiry? and How might I get the inquiry process started? To start an exploration of these questions, Lauren had arranged for Kathy Christensen, the state's 2009 Elementary Reading Coach of the Year, to address the coaches.

As Lauren knew she would, Kathy won over everyone with her enthusiasm. Kathy began by defining inquiry as "systematic, intentional study by educators of their own practice" and providing an overview of the five-step process: (1) developing a wondering, (2) collecting data, (3) analyzing data, (4) sharing, and (5) taking action for change and improvement. Kathy told stories of inquiry she had engaged in herself or had coached in her district. One powerful example she cited was about her whole faculty collaborating together on one schoolwide inquiry focused on the wondering,

"In what ways could our school's faculty increase the level of cognitive engagement among students?" To kick off this inquiry, in her dual role as reading coach and inquiry coach, Kathy described to the faculty the core elements of backward design in lesson planning. Next, each grade-level team worked together to develop an interdisciplinary unit using backward design; then they implemented the units in all classrooms, collected data on the impact of the units, and shared the results across grade levels in a subsequent faculty meeting. The impact on the school was profound. Teachers discovered the power of collaboration. As Kathy put it, "We discovered how much smarter we are together than any one of us is alone."

After providing an overview of the inquiry process and illustrating it with her own work, Kathy turned her talk to tips for coaches to get the inquiry process started among teachers. One tip, in particular, caused some laughter but resonated deeply with everyone.

> "COW stands for the Coalition of the Willing. These are teachers who welcome you . . ."

"Start with finding your COW," Kathy said. "Now, I would never use the term 'cow' to refer to any of my colleagues, but it is a great mnemonic device I use that reminds me of where to begin with my coaching work. COW stands for the Coalition of the Willing. These are teachers who welcome you, teachers with whom you already have a collegial relationship. Start with them because they are open to having you in their classrooms and willing to consider changes in their practice."

Kathy went on to explain the role coaches play in the process of inquiry. The coach helps a teacher or group of teachers define a wondering and develop a plan for the inquiry. She periodically reviews the work and student data with the teacher, and she provides ongoing feedback. Kathy ended her talk with what she believed to be the most important thing for coaches to keep in mind as they work. "Through the process of coaching inquiry, it's important to remember that the coach does not define the inquiry. For the teacher to grow professionally, the inquiry must be defined by the teacher and connect with her heart and soul. Therefore, often the coach's first and most important job is to be a good listener. By honoring teachers' interests and insights, I build trust. Trust and honor are essential to effective coaching."

There was a palpable excitement in the room as Kathy finished. And for the rest of the day and during subsequent meetings, when a coach began to talk about resistance or obstacles, someone would say, "Remember Kathy's advice; start with COW."

At the conclusion of the talk, Lauren thanked the guest speaker and instructed the group that after a short break, they would finish up their morning with an activity to help them think about how they could get inquiry started in their own contexts.

After the Break

Getting Started With Inquiry

Knowing that inquiry could be inspired by reflection on great teaching, Lauren and her planning team had decided to distribute a potentially useful resource to the group called *Secrets of Successful Teaching: Lessons From Award-Winning Teachers* (Ross et al., 2010). This paper describes the results of interviews with teachers in Florida who had been identified as demonstrating superior ability to help students achieve large gains in reading or math on the Florida Comprehensive Achievement Test (FCAT) and were subsequently honored by the Foundation for Excellence in Teaching with the Excel Award. Based on the interviews as well as a comprehensive review of research, the authors identified 14 "secrets of successful teaching" organized into three categories: building a relationship for success, developing a community of learning, and techniques that work.

Building a Relationship for Success

Secret 1: Nurture an authentic relationship of respect and caring.
Secret 2: Hold students to high expectations.
Secret 3: Convey an unwavering belief in your students' ability to achieve.
Secret 4: Celebrate progress but keep raising the bar.

Developing a Community of Learning

Secret 5: Set clear guidelines for conduct in the classroom.
Secret 6: Foster an atmosphere in which it is safe to take academic risks.
Secret 7: Make your classroom an engaging place.

Teaching Techniques That Work

Secret 8: Tailor instruction to meet the needs of every student.
Secret 9: Use multiple methods throughout the year to assess students' knowledge.
Secret 10: Adapt instruction based upon the results of assessments.
Secret 11: Relate learning to "real" life.
Secret 12: Orchestrate, don't control.
Secret 13: Get beyond the basics of who, what, where, and when.
Secret 14: Prepare for formal testing, but focus on learning for life.

Feedback Carousel Protocol

In the next segment of the meeting, Lauren modeled the ways this resource might be used with potential inquirers to help them define their inquiries by adapting a protocol called "Feedback Carousel" (http://nsrfharmony.org/protocol/doc/feed_back_carousel.pdf).

After the break, Lauren explained to the group that she had selected the next protocol and activity for two reasons. First, it would prompt a discussion about effective teaching practice,

> "Surfacing dilemmas is the foundation to developing a good wondering for any inquiry."

and according to Lauren, "Effective teaching practice is the foundation upon which all inquiry is based." Second, the coaches could use the activity in their own contexts to not only create an opportunity for teachers to discuss their practice, but to help them surface dilemmas they face. And, Lauren shared, "Surfacing dilemmas is the foundation to developing a good wondering for any inquiry."

To move expeditiously through the "secrets of successful teaching" publication, the group divided up the material, with each person reading one secret. People were assigned a number from 1 to 14, read the secret that corresponded to their number, and then gathered in an area of the room with the other members of the group who had the same number and had read the same secret. As everyone moved into their small groups, Lauren and her team circulated about the room handing each group a piece of chart paper and a set of markers.

Lauren announced, "Now it's time to bring out your artistic and creative side as your group illustrates the meaning of your secret of success. You have 10 minutes to discuss and illustrate your secret. Make sure your illustration is labeled with the name of your secret and reflects your notes, key findings, and any important points that surfaced in your conversation about your piece of the text." Figure 8.2 shows two of the illustrations the coaches produced.

As each group talked about and illustrated the meaning of their assigned "secret," Lauren circulated the room again, placing one or two packages of post-it notes by every group. As the illustrations were finished and posted around the room, Lauren explained that next everyone needed to move around the room in silence to read each group's chart. They were to use post-it notes to write down any potential questions or wonderings related to that secret and post them by the secret. The group had five minutes to silently visit and comment on as many of the secrets as possible. After five minutes, everyone returned to his or her own secret, read the post-it notes by their secret, discussed these with each other, and prepared a one-minute summary of the secret and the questions posed.

Next, Lauren asked for a group to volunteer to speak first. Group 4 volunteered. "Our secret was 'Celebrate progress but keep raising the bar.' In relation to this secret, our group talked about how it is important to challenge students, but at the same time, recognize that students don't arrive to us as blank slates, so not every child needs the same type of challenge. Rather, kids arrive to us with different levels of prior success and with different gaps in

Figure 8.2   Examples of "Secrets" Illustrated

their knowledge and skills. As teachers, we need to decide definitively that we will not 'teach down' to students who struggle, but rather provide whatever it takes to support their success. I quote from our reading, 'Of course, some students do not initially believe in themselves nor succeed in their first efforts to meet the standards. It is critical that teachers respond to students' struggles appropriately. When teachers steadfastly believe in students, students begin to believe in themselves' (Ross et al., 2010, p. 8). This statement really resonated with our group. In addition, our group found the questions that were written on the post-it notes to be provocative:

- Why should every child have to celebrate the same accomplishments like honor roll or perfect attendance?
- What do students want to celebrate?
- What happens if we ask the students what they want to celebrate?
- What happens if students set their own goals and we celebrate their making those goals?
- How can we keep 'raising the bar' incrementally in response to student needs without being overwhelmed by the need to cover material for the FCAT? In other words, how do we use the test as a target for raising the bar for struggling students over time without letting the test 'take' us as teachers?

These questions helped us dig deeper into the meaning of this secret, and we can see how this would be a powerful tool to help teachers generate ideas for inquiry."

Reports by the 13 remaining groups followed, with each group agreeing that the activity could spur wonderful discussions about genuine dilemmas and questions of practice. To debrief the activity as a whole group, Lauren asked the coaches to think about the impact the "Feedback Carousel" activity might have back in their own schools. One administrator shared, "I think I'd like to do this activity at one of my first faculty meetings of the school year. When I do this at my school, I want to make sure the posters are left in a place where teachers can review their thinking and notes because I think we will generate great ideas for inquiry that we will want to revisit." Another member of the group, who had engaged in inquiry with her grade-level team in the past, commented, "This was so much easier and more fun than just sitting around trying to come up with an idea for an inquiry project. We all had ideas about the secrets, and we built on each other's comments." Finally, one coach summed it up, "You just couldn't help but have ideas and thoughts about those 14 secrets of teaching. All of us have a vested interest in doing whatever it takes to help our students. As we talked with each other, our ideas evolved and the energy in our group was contagious. I can't wait to take this experience back to the teachers at my school."

AFTER LUNCH

Coaching Wondering Development

Lauren used the afternoon session to focus on the art of providing feedback as a coach, particularly in relation to the very first step of the inquiry process: developing a good question or wondering. To do so, Lauren shared the story of Greg, an effective inquiry coach and Steve, a teacher starting the process of inquiry, from *The Reflective Educator's Guide to Professional Development: Coaching Inquiry-Oriented Learning Communities* (Dana & Yendol-Hoppey, 2008). Before Lauren began reading to the group, she asked them to listen for positive actions the coach in the story takes to make the feedback process a positive experience for Steve.

A Feedback Experience

Steve's passion for teaching high school chemistry caught fire with his participation in a professional learning community at his school. He especially enjoyed interacting with other teachers outside of the science department, and found that listening to their experiences teaching other subject areas (English, Spanish, Math, Geometry, and Biology) offered him a fresh perspective on his own teaching of chemistry. Last year, his PLC members helped Steve craft an inquiry that helped him look deeply at the use of lecture demonstrations to empower student learning. Steve learned a great deal about his

(Continued)

(Continued)

practice through engaging in this inquiry and was even invited to present his research at his state's annual science teacher meeting. This school year, Steve's PLC decided to again support each other in the teacher research they would conduct into their own classrooms. Steve was looking forward to another cycle of inquiry.

Knowing that this PLC not only worked well together, but also enjoyed each other's company, PLC facilitator and English teacher, Greg, suggested that the group meet Friday afternoon at 4:00 at a local bar to share and discuss their potential questions for exploration through inquiry. Greg affectionately referred to this meeting as, "Our Wondering Happy Hour." The group agreed that it would be a nice, relaxed way to get them moving on their research.

In between chicken wings and sips of beer, group members each took a turn talking about their questions. Greg looked at Steve, "We haven't heard from you yet. What are you thinking about for this year?"

Steve began, "I've been thinking about my assessment strategies, especially the tests I give. I'm thinking of doing something focused on my students' performance on these tests . . . maybe do an item analysis, or something like that."

Greg noticed from Steve's body language and tone of voice that the same enthusiasm evident throughout Steve's inquiry the previous year was not present. Greg invited Steve to elaborate on his thinking: "Tell me more."

"The tests just don't feel right to me, so it might help to analyze their content."

Greg continued, "What would you expect to learn about your students from this inquiry?"

"I'm not sure what I'd learn about my students from analyzing the tests, but I can tell you something about the students I teach. There's a small group of kids that rely extremely heavily on my extra-help sessions. Because they know I offer these sessions, as the school requires us to do, they don't pay attention when I introduce a concept to be tested in class—instead they figure they can pick it up in the extra-help session."

Greg noticed Steve was becoming more and more animated as he talked about the extra-help sessions. Steve continued, "Often in Chemistry, my students are overwhelmed with the complexity of learning such an abstract science. They often enter my class having heard stories from their parents about the horrors of college chemistry classes. Many have notions that chemistry is something that will be impossible for them to learn. I, as a chemistry teacher, realize that the subject will be more easily understood by some students than others. Many of my students honestly need help outside of the normal class in order to achieve an acceptable grade. Help sessions are a place where students can get the help they need. Yet, what I have noticed is that many of these students rely on these out of class help sessions to be a place where they can learn the concepts that I have already taught in class itself. As a result, some of my students are off task during class because they feel like they can learn the material in the help session anyhow. Why do they need to pay attention during class?"

Greg responded, "It seems to me that the tests themselves are not what you are really interested in exploring, but the help sessions to prepare students for the test."

"Yes," Steve replied, "that's it. More specifically, I would like to examine my students' perceptions of help sessions. I feel like maybe a different perspective would be beneficial both to them as students and to myself as their teacher. I think that help sessions should be better termed "office hours." Students should come to these office hours to seek answers to questions, not to be taught concepts that have already been covered in class."

Greg grabbed his notepad and said, "Let's jot down those ideas before we lose them." On the pad, Greg wrote the phrases, "Understanding Student Perceptions of Help Session," and "Getting a Different Perspective on Help Sessions." Steve worked some more on that paper, playing with questions to frame his inquiry. When he left the happy hour that evening, he read through the scribbling on his notepad:

- What is the most productive way to structure after-school help?
- What are students' perceptions and expectations for extra help?
- How does one create a student-driven vs. teacher-driven after school session?
- What is the relationship between misbehavior during class and attendance at after school help?
- What skills do my students need to take charge of their extra help?
- What is the chemistry skill level of my students who seek help outside of class?
- Are these help times increasing the knowledge of my chemistry students?

Steve believed he had a great start to wondering development, and was excited to get this inquiry underway! (pp. 71–73)

At the conclusion of the story, people worked in small groups to discuss and analyze the particulars of Greg's feedback actions as a coach. Then, as a whole group they discussed some of the things they had noticed in the story. One person said, "We talked about how keenly Greg observed Steve's body language as he was talking. Through this observation he realized that Steve was initially going in the direction of something he wasn't really passionate about exploring."

From another group someone added, "We noticed the same thing in our group, and what we admired was that Greg didn't blurt, 'I can tell from your body language that you don't care very deeply about this topic. You should think about something different!' Rather, Greg simply invited Steve to elaborate by saying 'Tell me more.'"

A third group chimed in, "That gave Greg, as coach, the opportunity to listen and be able to tell whether his initial deduction was accurate about Steve's topic not being something he was passionate about exploring. It's like our speaker said this morning, 'Often the coach's first and most important job is to be a good listener.'"

Another group added, "We thought an important thing Greg did was ask a good probing question: 'What would you expect to learn about your students from this inquiry?' As Steve answered this question, he saw for himself that he wasn't really hot on doing an item analysis of his tests."

Lauren summed up, "Through Greg's patient, careful listening and questioning, he drew out the burning question about practice that Steve had—another phrase our keynoter used this morning." Lauren then asked that each group give her one feedback principle that arose out of their discussion of the reading. The groups started the following list:

- Be patient.
- Listen carefully.
- Ask good clarifying and probing questions.
- Be honest about your position or limitations.

BRINGING CLOSURE TO THE DAY

It was almost the end of the day. Coaches had been inspired by the words of a gifted inquiry coach; they had worked through a process to get teachers talking about their practice and generate general topics for exploration through inquiry; they had thought about and established a set of principles for delivering effective feedback. They spent the rest of their afternoon planning their approach to inquiry in their individual contexts.

At 2:45, Lauren called the group back together to bring closure to the day by explaining how the rest of the coaching series would unfold over the course of the year. At their October meeting, the group would review data collection strategies for practitioner inquirers. In addition, they would look at examples of inquiry briefs (a one- or two-page plan for inquiry) as well as an inquiry template that the coaches might like to use to help their coaches plan their inquiries. (Inquiry brief examples and the inquiry template are available on the companion website to this book).

At the January meeting, the group would work on data analysis, particularly as it related to ways to organize and make sense of qualitative data (i.e., data other than test scores and grades that did not take the form of numbers). Lauren explained that qualitative data such as classroom observations, student work, journaling, and interviewing frequently played a large part in practitioner inquiry but were often the kinds of data that teachers needed the most help analyzing. At the January meeting Lauren and the coaches would also discuss the details of the district's first inquiry showcase and how to prepare for this event.

After the inquiry showcase in April, the group would meet one final time in May to look at the results of a feedback survey that would be given to all inquiry showcase attendees. Further, the group would review their work for the year and set goals for the future.

After examining the calendar, Lauren invited the coaches to complete a feedback form that contained four questions:

1. What is one significant learning you are taking away from our session today?

2. What was the best part of today's session?

3. What would have helped you learn more from today's session?

4. What questions or concerns do you still have about coaching inquiry this year?

Back at central office, Lauren and her staff reviewed the feedback. Feedback was overwhelmingly positive and Day 1 of the Coaches Series was a success. Although there was a good deal of work ahead to transform the delivery of professional development in their district, they knew coaching would play a huge role in their efforts. After the first day, they were off to a strong start.

Questions for Discussion

Part IV: For the Professional Developer

Part IV of this text focused on the coach's role in building a successful districtwide professional development plan. Reflect on Part IV and apply what you've learned from the two chapters to your own context by answering the following questions:

1. Lauren used a protocol called "Block Party" to get people from different schools across the district to meet one another and engage them in an initial discussion about inquiry. In what ways could you adapt the block party protocol to use with teachers? With principals? With students?

2. Lauren developed an activity based on a reading called *Secrets of Successful Teaching* to kick off the coaches' discussion about getting inquiry started in their schools.

   - Do you think this was an effective activity for this purpose? Why or why not?
   - Which of the secrets of success do you believe to be most important for your district or school to target at this particular time?
   - What actions might you take to target these secrets?

3. The guest speaker, Kathy, discussed the importance of COW— Coalition of the Willing.

   - Who are the COW in your district or school?
   - How might you engage them in the development of a system-wide district professional development plan?
   - How do you handle the opposite of COW—people in your district who are cynical and negative?
   - What reasons do you believe cynics would give for their skepticism about job-embedded professional development?
   - How do you prevent cynics from undermining your district's efforts to develop a powerful systemwide professional development plan?

4. What do you feel would be the greatest benefit to establishing a cadre of formal and informal coaches across your district and/or strengthening the coaching practice of coaches you already have?

5. What do you feel would be the greatest challenge to establishing a cadre of formal and informal coaches across your district and/or strengthening the practice of coaches you already have? How might these challenges be addressed?

Conclusion

Pulling the Pieces Together

A District Culture of Inquiry

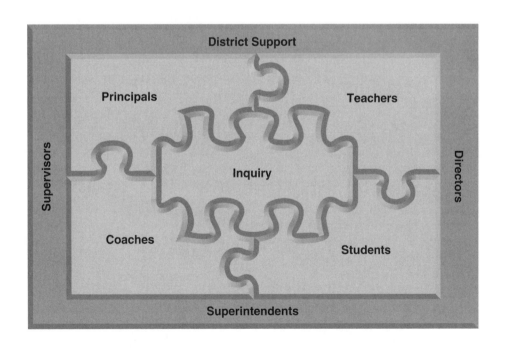

Pulling the
Pieces Together

A District Culture of Inquiry

Cultures of inquiry create a risk-taking, experimental environment that encourages members to develop, reflect on, and modify structures and processes. The larger system must not penalize such risk-taking by creating a high-stakes environment or imposing highly structured or constrained settings for change. Instead, it should support, encourage, and reward open-ended, creative work.

—Kathleen Cushman (1999)

In the preface to this book, we introduced the notion that the creation of a comprehensive, systematic, professional development program that targets the learning of all adult and student members and spans an entire district is a daunting and complex task, and we likened it to putting together a very intricate and complicated jigsaw puzzle. Hence, we used a jigsaw puzzle image—a visual metaphor—to organize and illustrate the contents of this book. As this text comes to a close, we now have all the puzzle pieces in place:

- Inquiry (the central piece of the puzzle that ties all learning in the district together);
- Principals, teachers, and students (the people who benefit, learn, and grow from engagement in inquiry); and
- Coaches (the people who create the learning conditions ripe for inquiry to unfold in classrooms and schools districtwide).

Although the puzzle pieces are now all in place, it's important to note that puzzles are fragile things. Once a puzzle is completed, it can't be easily moved from one place to another without falling apart. For this reason, puzzles (especially those intended for small children), often contain a frame within which the puzzle can be assembled. The frame serves as a structure to keep the pieces together and keep the puzzle whole.

As alluded to in the opening quote to this concluding chapter, in the case of our puzzle, the frame is the larger system—the district. The larger system must support, encourage, and reward all constituencies in the district who are engaging in the important work of learning. In particular, central office administration (superintendents, directors, and supervisors) serves as the glue that holds all the pieces in a successful districtwide professional development plan puzzle together.

The voice of central office administration is critical to the continued growth and development of inquiry-focused professional development. The district leadership must articulate a clear vision of what powerful professional development looks and feels like districtwide and send a persistent message that learning is the important job of *everyone* in the district—principals, teachers, students, and central office administrators. An effective way to send this message is to have district leaders themselves begin to study their own professional practice, reinforcing the message that educator inquiry is the foundation of all professional learning and necessary to improve the learning and life opportunities for *every* student. According to Cushman (1999),

> A culture of inquiry is an "open system," continually examining its own purposes as well as the ways it reaches those purposes. New and even conflicting ideas can come into the system at any time to influence what happens. The school's vision guides its work, but in a dynamic tension with its actions, each tested against the other in an ongoing inquiry into the current state of affairs.

Frequently district administrators choose to study the very processes of professional development described in this book at a systems level. For example, in Pinellas County Schools (PCS), the Cabinet (consisting of the superintendent; deputy superintendent; six area superintendents; the assistant superintendents of human resources, management information systems, finance, curriculum and instruction, and exceptional student education; and three directors) is about to launch a collaborative inquiry framed by the wondering, "What happens when Pinellas County Schools shifts the emphasis for professional development from district-led events to job-embedded learning through inquiry?" Subquestions include the following:

- What is the relationship between this shift in emphasis and teacher satisfaction with professional development?
- What is the relationship between this shift in emphasis and administrator satisfaction with professional development?

- What is the relationship between this shift in emphasis and student achievement?
- In what ways does the "system" need to adjust and change as professional development efforts become job-embedded?

By embarking on this shared inquiry journey, PCS district leaders live the process of inquiry alongside the principals, teachers, and students in their charge, demonstrating another core feature of an inquiry culture discussed by Cushman (1999):

> Rather than asking how to make a current structure more efficient or how to put a new one into practice, inquiry cultures ask what problems the old structures solved, what values they reflected, whose interests they served, what structures might be more consistent with the values and beliefs of the school's vision, and what people need to know to enact those. An inflexible, prescriptive bureaucratic system does not work well with this; instead, the larger system also must be able to purposefully reconfigure itself as necessary.

By embarking on this shared inquiry journey, PCS district leaders are enabling their school system to reconfigure itself in response to principal, teacher, and student needs.

In addition to this shared, collaborative inquiry, the superintendent and deputy superintendent of PCS model for their Cabinet and for every teacher, administrator, and student in their district the power of learning through inquiry by engaging in inquiry themselves and making their learning and leading both public and transparent. For example, at the kick-off retreat for more than 400 PCS administrators at the start of the school year, Julie Janssen and Jim Madden told the assembled group that after listening to the morning speaker who discussed the power of job-embedded learning through inquiry and engaging in activities with everyone present at the retreat, they realized that they needed to model the same types of learning they were expecting everyone in the district to engage in that school year. They announced that they were about to embark on a study of their practice as superintendent and deputy superintendent in relation to school board meetings. They wondered how the use of protocols at board meetings might impact the dialogue and discussion that occurs there. They planned to try a protocol at the next board meeting and collect data on what transpires as they put into practice the same structures they were hoping teachers and administrators would use to structure their meeting and professional learning time. In this way, Julie and Jim modeled professional learning and growth at its best. Their actions as inquirers spoke louder than any words they could ever deliver to the administrators in the district that day.

In sum, a solid frame within which to assemble a successful district-wide professional development plan puzzle consists of the district leadership creating a culture of inquiry that supports, encourages, and rewards learning for *all*. Modeling the process of inquiry in genuine and authentic ways is one powerful method district leaders can use to create this culture. As district leaders work alongside principals, teachers, and students within this culture, they will learn many lessons about education as well as many lessons about what it takes to build a powerful systemwide professional development program. To kick off this learning, we close this book with our own "One Dozen Lessons Learned," derived from looking at all the content and stories shared in this book as well as our own experiences working in schools and school systems that have created a culture of inquiry.

One Dozen Lessons for Building a Successful Districtwide Professional Development Program

> **Lesson 1: Establishing structures and processes (such as learning communities, community norms, and protocols) lays an essential foundation for job-embedded learning through inquiry districtwide.**

Throughout the stories in this book, learning communities (small groups of educators who meet regularly to engage in collaborative, professional dialogue with one another about their practice) serve as the "containers" for professional learning through inquiry. The meeting time of learning communities is highly structured to ensure deliberate dialogue by teachers and principals about student work and student learning. Because the experience of engaging in deliberative professional dialogue focused intently on student work and student learning is unfamiliar to most educators, it is critical in learning communities to spend time developing a set of community norms (agreements for how learning community members will work together) as well as to use protocols (a series of timed steps that guide how a conversation will unfold).

Community Norms

Community norms set parameters for learning community members' behavior to provide teachers, coaches, and administrators with opportunities to freely grapple with real-life dilemmas. Identifying the way the group will work and holding people accountable for following the norms is a worthwhile investment because it provides a secure environment that encourages people to share freely. As we learned from the stories of Carol, Bob, and Sylvia (Chapter 2) and The GIRLS (Chapter 4), the following are typical community agreements:

- Speak and listen from the heart (the goal is understanding, not agreement),
- Monitor equity of participation,
- Acknowledge one another as equals,
- Assume goodwill,
- Trust the process,
- Be present (on time, cell phones/BlackBerries off, in the room), and
- Expect it to get messy at times.

Community agreements are a necessary structure for the important work of inquiry to create a safe space for learning community members to make themselves professionally vulnerable to one another. Because inquiry emerges from real-world dilemmas and felt difficulties of practice, making oneself vulnerable to others is a necessary part of the work, but it can only occur when the environment feels safe.

Protocols

Protocols provide a predictable, organized set of steps to follow to ensure that discussions promote meaningful and efficient communication. A number of different protocols were utilized throughout this book:

Chapter 2: The Story of Carol, Sylvia, Bob, and 37 Principals

- The Four A's
- Forming Ground Rules
- Making Meaning
- KWL
- Text Rendering

Chapter 4: The Story of the GIRLS

- Creating Metaphors
- Passions Profile
- Check-in Circle
- Consultancy
- Data-Driven Dialogue

Chapter 8: The Story of Lauren, Professional Development Director

- Block Party
- Feedback Carousel

Each of the protocols described in this text was selected and utilized for a variety of reasons and purposes, including the following:

- Dealing with issues and dilemmas related to educator learning,
- Looking closely at and learning from educator work and/or student data,
- Scaffolding peer observations and debriefing, and
- Learning from written texts.

Whatever the reason for their selection and use, it is clear from looking at all the stories shared in this book that protocols serve to concentrate conversation on professional practice and to keep conversation from straying into areas unrelated to teaching and learning. In addition, the use of protocols helps ensure that everyone has the opportunity to participate in dialogue; no one community member can dominate "air time," and no one community member can sit back in silence. These are very significant benefits of protocol use and demonstrate its importance in the inquiry process districtwide. Indeed, Carol used protocols to structure conversation among principals, Kathy used protocols to structure conversation among teachers, Lauren used protocols to structure conversation among coaches, and as we learn in this chapter, Superintendent Julie Janssen and Deputy Superintendent Jim Madden used protocols to structure conversation among school board members.

Because protocols serve such a vital function districtwide, it is important for members in the district representing all different constituencies to become intimately familiar with the range of protocols available from such organizations as the National School Reform Faculty as well as to become skilled facilitators in their use. For this purpose, we highly recommend that designated teachers, principals, and central office administrators spend time in facilitation training by the National School Reform Faculty or a similar organization.

> **Lesson 2: National professional organizations provide tremendous support for envisioning, enacting, and sustaining a powerful districtwide professional development plan.**

Establishing a systemwide approach to professional development that simultaneously targets the enhancement of teacher quality and student achievement through job-embedded learning is complicated work. It is difficult for a district to be successful if it tries to establish and sustain a professional development plan on its own. Fortunately, a number of wonderful organizations can provide support and resources for districts as they transform themselves into vibrant learning organizations. The educators in this book all drew energy and knowledge from national organizations such as Learning Forward (formally the National Staff Development Council), National School Reform Faculty, and Coalition of Essential Schools. We recommend taking the time to connect to some entity larger than an individual district to support the entire system in the creation of powerful learning opportunities for all its members.

Lesson 3: Time is a significant factor to consider when building a systematic, successful district professional development plan.

Taking the time to connect to a larger national organization is important, but not sufficient, to build a successful districtwide professional development plan. Time must be spent in other ways as well: learning about the process of inquiry, meeting in various learning community configurations across the district to engage in inquiry, finding resources and reading to support inquiry work, and creating an opportunity for the learning that is occurring in smaller communities of practice across the district to cross-pollinate at events such as the Inquiry Celebration (Chapter 2), the Inquiry Expo (Chapter 4), or the Inquiry Showcase (Chapter 6). The educators in the stories in this book all understood the time it takes to create a successful districtwide professional development program and found ways to restructure time during administrators' and teachers' contracted school days to create opportunities for professional learning to occur not as an "add on" to an already very full plate, but as a natural and necessary part of the way the business of learning is done in the district.

The issue of time is, and always will be, unchanging. No one ever has enough of it and everyone wishes for more. Yet, for a districtwide professional development plan to be a success, time *must* be invested in the process. Although time must be invested, districts yield a much higher return rate on time invested in this form of professional learning than in the "one-shot deal" alone (Desimone, 2009).

Lesson 4: Building a districtwide professional development program that works takes both patience and persistence.

Because building a successful districtwide professional development program takes time, it also calls for patience. The entire system cannot transform itself overnight, in a few weeks, in a few months, or even in a year.

Patience means being willing to start slowly and allow the power of job-embedded learning to reveal itself to all members of the district over time. In Chapter 2, Carol, Sylvia, and Bob spent an entire school year focused solely on helping principals in their region engage in

administrator inquiry, so they could experience what powerful professional learning felt like. After the story presented in this book, Carol,
Sylvia, and Bob spent another entire year with their principals, focused on
coaching inquiry. It was only during their second year of work together
that Carol expected the principals to actively encourage and support this
way of working in their own schools.

Patience also means being willing to slow the work down at times. For
example, when Carol, Sylvia, and Bob received feedback from their principal advisory group that principals were confused about the purpose and
steps of inquiry, they took a step back and created opportunities for the
principals to learn more about the inquiry process itself, rather than continuing to push the development of the principals' inquiries forward.
Building a districtwide professional development program that works
often means taking one step back in order to take two steps forward.

Although it is important to demonstrate patience, it is just as important
to demonstrate persistence. When something takes time or needs to be
slowed down, it's easy to abandon the effort. Persistence means developing a clearly articulated vision and continuing to share that vision widely
and frequently so that everyone stays the course.

> **Lesson 5: Building a districtwide professional development program that works is both exhilarating and exhausting.**

Staying the course over time takes energy. There is no doubt that all the
educators in this book expended a great deal of energy on their own professional learning as well as on the professional learning of their
colleagues. When one's professional learning tightly wraps around the
learning of students, there is an intensity to the work that is unlike anything many educators have ever experienced. Although this intensity can
be exhausting, it is also exhilarating. Mike Feeney, assistant principal at
Oldsmar Elementary School in the Pinellas County Schools, shares,

> I remember sitting with other assistant principals and talking
> about moving inquiry forward in our schools. We all agreed that it
> was not only physically exhausting, but at the end of many of our
> learning community meetings where we discussed our own and
> our teachers' inquiries, we were emotionally and mentally drained.
> We all admitted that helping teachers think about, discuss, and
> investigate their practice was incredibly demanding work for an
> administrator. As school administrators, it was much easier to just
> hand over a solution. Discovering the possibilities of a "new prac-
> tice" was more difficult and definitely more tiring than implement-
> ing initiatives and monitoring mandates.

However, as we were talking I couldn't help but smile as I recalled the vision of one of my fifth-grade teachers bouncing around her class with huge amounts of energy and passion as she worked on her inquiry project with her students. She bubbled, "I'm making my wondering real!" as she had tried a new math strategy that had ignited her students' enthusiasm for compound fractions. The room was energized, and when it was time to end the math lesson the students booed! The teacher couldn't get the students to stop doing math problems, and the teacher didn't want to stop teaching mathematics.

I realized that my teacher's belief that she was a learner who was in control of her learning was contagious. Not only had her students caught the fever, but so had many of her colleagues. I decided that this was the type of exhaustion every administrator should experience!

> **Lesson 6: Fluidity and flexibility must be woven into the fabric of the districtwide professional development plan.**

One of the reasons exhilaration can grow from exhaustion is that inquiry is a cycle, not a linear progression of rigid steps that everyone in the district follows in a lock-step manner. Educators can jump into the cycle at any point, at any time. Because there is fluidity built into the cycle of inquiry, the learning that occurs cannot help but be meaningful; the cycle continual adjusts itself for each individual as the process of inquiry unfolds. Questions can morph as data are collected and indicate a new direction for learning. New questions emerge as one cycle of inquiry ends and another one begins. Meaningful learning is the source of feelings of exhilaration generated by this fluid, cyclical process.

Because of the fluidity built into the cycle of inquiry, for a districtwide professional development program to be successful, flexibility is key. Flexibility means that you may have lots of different people and different configurations of people engaged in the cycle of inquiry in different places and times at any point in a school year. And, because an entire system cannot be transformed all at once, flexibility also means allowing educators to be introduced to the process of inquiry incrementally. This means recognizing that all members of the district will be in different places in relation to their development as inquirers. Hence, in addition to creating the space for all educators across the district to engage in the process, it is important for districts to provide opportunities for the continual development and refinement of the skills associated with inquiry. There is no "one size fits all" approach to learning about inquiry. Flexibility must be built into the entire system to adapt to the needs of educators in different places and phases in their professional development as both educators and inquirers.

> **Lesson 7: The quality of inquiry improves with time and experience.**

It is unlikely that district administrators hold the same classroom teaching performance expectations for a novice teacher as they do for a 25-year veteran. Likewise, it is unlikely the first time a teacher, principal, or central office administrator engages in practitioner inquiry he or she will excel at every aspect of the inquiry process. Yet, first-time practitioner-researcher attempts at inquiry should be met with encouragement, support, and positive reinforcement. As one teacher noted, "Don't ever, ever criticize the work of a first-time inquirer. . . . I know where I can improve and I will take everything I've learned into my next inquiry."

The quality of teacher inquiry improves with experience. Many first-time inquirers are timid and choose to limit their inquiries to issues they already have thought about, and they even may have identified resources to help them resolve the dilemma. To an observer, these seemingly superficial inquiries appear to be of limited value. However, over time, teacher inquirers tackle increasingly difficult challenges and step further outside their comfort zones. Their questions become profound, their outside resources improve in quality, and their designs for their inquiries become sophisticated. As teachers and administrators become experts at inquiry, the rigor and clarity of their inquiries increase significantly. Those engaging in inquiry (including professional development personnel) should consider the first year of inquiry as a learning journey—discovering the power of inquiry, of collaboration, and of collective wisdom.

> **Lesson 8: Collaboration unleashes learning potential and plays a vital role in job-embedded professional development.**

Collaboration was evident throughout every story in this text:

- Carol collaborated with Sylvia, Bob, and the Principal Advisory Group to better understand the needs of the 37 principals with whom she worked as the principals in this story collaborated with one another on inquiry (Chapter 2);
- The GIRLS collaborated with one another to explore the relationship between different pedagogical strategies they were employing in science instruction and the development of their ESL students' science content vocabulary (Chapter 4);

- Teachers at the elementary level (Judi and Marcia), the middle school level (Randi and Wendy), and the high school level (Jeanette and Julie) collaborated to engage their students as inquirers (Chapter 6);
- Lauren collaborated with other members in the PD department as well as educators in her district who had a great deal of experience with inquiry to develop a cadre of coaches in her district (Chapter 8).

In all these cases, learning was both deepened and accelerated through the process of collaboration. In fact, much of the learning that occurred in these stories would never have happened if any one of these individuals had been working in isolation. Collaboration serves as a catalyst for learning.

> **Lesson 9: The development of a successful districtwide professional development plan depends upon modeling, modeling, modeling, and modeling again.**

Just as collaboration serves as a catalyst for learning, modeling serves as a catalyst for job-embedded learning through inquiry to transfer to different contexts in the district simultaneously, thereby speeding up the adoption of inquiry as the way of work districtwide. Modeling means using the same processes that promote powerful learning opportunities in all contexts, and perhaps more important, purposefully debriefing the learning opportunities and asking participants to discuss how the processes they experienced might transfer to their own context. In Chapter 2, at the end of every regional meeting, Carol purposefully asked the principals how they might utilize "The 4 A's," "Forming Ground Rules," "Making Meaning," and "KWL" back at their schools. In Chapter 4, Kathy asked the teachers in her learning community how they might adapt "Creating Metaphors" and "Consultancy" to use with the students in their own classrooms. In Chapter 6, Lauren asked the coaches how they might adapt "Block Party" and "Feedback Carousel" for use in their own coaching contexts. As a result of purposeful debriefing of modeling, participants begin to see the ways their own powerful experiences as learners can be transferred to their work as administrators or teachers. In fact, this is one significant reason the process of inquiry as a mechanism for adult learning has been translated into a mechanism for student learning in the classroom as well.

> **Lesson 10: When powerful learning conditions for adults are created and established in a district, the creation of powerful learning experiences for students naturally follows.**

Part III of this book explicates the ways students in a district can be powerfully engaged as learners through inquiry. In the elementary, middle school, and high school stories exemplifying students as inquirers in Chapter 6, every teacher was inspired to engage students as inquirers as a result of his or her own engagement in the process of inquiry as adult learners. Whether adult or student, engagement in the process of inquiry makes learning immediate, relevant, self-directed, collaborative, engaging, and last but not least, differentiated.

> **Lesson 11: Inquiry provides an effective way to differentiate instruction for every learner in the district—adults and students alike.**

Differentiated instruction aims to make visible individual student needs that can become lost in traditional school structures (Tomlinson, 1999, 2001). According to Hall (2002),

> differentiated instruction applies an approach to teaching and learning so that students have multiple options for taking in information and making sense of ideas. The model of differentiated instruction requires teachers to be flexible in their approach to teaching and adjusting the curriculum and presentation of information to learners rather than expecting students to modify themselves for the curriculum.

By engaging in inquiry, teachers can generate valuable knowledge about their learners' readiness, interest, learning styles, and more. With this knowledge, teachers make adaptations to instruction, increasing the probability that the needs of *all* learners will be met in a single class period or lesson. In fact, engaging students as inquirers is one way to differentiate instruction to meet the needs of every learner. In the words of Sharon Earle, a teacher whose students engaged in inquiry as described in Chapter 5 of this book, "We have so many needs in our classroom. Inquiry met the needs of the lowest students but also kept the highest students engaged."

Just as students in Sharon's classroom had many different instructional needs, teachers and administrators in any district have many different professional development needs that could never begin to be addressed in a stand-alone, one-day workshop. Just as different student needs in Sharon's classroom were met simultaneously through inquiry, the different professional development needs of principals and teachers across a district can be met simultaneously through inquiry as well. Inquiry provides an effective mechanism not only to differentiate instruction for students by classroom teachers, but to differentiate professional development for teachers and administrators across a district.

Lesson 12: It takes a district to teach a child!

For our final lesson, we come full circle, ending our book as we began it. In the introduction to our text, we adapted the ancient African proverb "It takes a village to raise a child" to "It takes a district to teach a child." Unfortunately, many districts and educators across the nation continue to search for one silver bullet that will quickly and definitively enhance teacher quality and raise student achievement in every classroom and in every school. We illustrate with the rich stories of real educators in this book that there does not exist one such solution. Rather, it will take the work of us all—principals, teachers, students, coaches, and central office administration. The efforts of all these stakeholders are brought together as districts develop a systems approach to learning grounded in inquiry. And, we have learned from the educators in this book, when a district takes a systems approach to learning that is grounded in inquiry, it works! It really does take a district to teach a child.

References

Adams, A., Ross, D. D., Swain, C., Dana, N. F., Leite, W., & Sandbach, R. (2011). *Preparing teacher leaders in job-embedded graduate programs: Changes within and beyond the classroom walls.* Paper presented at the annual meeting of the American Educational Research Association, New Orleans, LA.

Barkley, S. G. (2005). *Quality teaching in a culture of coaching.* Lanham, MD: Scarecrow Education.

Barth, R. (1990). *Improving schools from within: Teachers, parents, and principals can make the difference.* San Francisco: Jossey-Bass.

Barth, R. (2001). Principal centered professional development. *Theory Into Practice, 25*(3), 156–160.

Bell, R. L., Smetana, L., & Binns, I. (2005). Simplifying inquiry instruction. *The Science Teacher,* 30–33.

Brickman, J. (2010). *Lesson ideas to enrich student inquiry into the Holocaust.* Scholastic.com. Retrieved from http://www2.scholastic.com/browse/lessonplan.jsp?id=395

Brickman, P., Gormally, C., Armstrong, N., & Hallar, B. (2009). Effects of inquiry-based learning on students' science literacy skills and confidence. *International Journal for the Scholarship of Teaching and Learning, 3*(2). Retrieved from http://www.georgiasouthern.edu/ijsotl

Brookfield, S. (1992). Developing criteria for formal theory building in adult education. *Adult Education Quarterly, 42*(2), 79–93.

Bundy, A. L. (2005). Aligning systems to create full-service schools: The Boston experience, so far. *New Directions for Youth Development, 107,* 73–80.

Byrne-Jimenez, M., & Orr, M. T. (2007). *Developing effective principals through collaborative inquiry.* New York: Teachers College Press.

Callison, D. (1999). Key words, concepts and methods for information age instruction: A guide to teaching information literacy. *School Library Media Activities Monthly, 15*(6), 38–42.

Caro-Bruce, C., Flessner, R., Klehr, M., & Zeichner, K. M. (2007). *Creating equitable classrooms through action research.* Thousand Oaks, CA: Corwin.

Carr, W., & Kemmis, S. (1986). *Becoming critical: Knowing through action research.* Geelong, Victoria, Australia: Deakin University Press.

Center for Science, Mathematics, and Engineering Education. (2000). *Inquiry and the National Science Standards: A guide for teaching and learning.* Washington, DC: National Academy Press.

Check, J. (1997). Teacher research as powerful professional development. *Harvard Education Letter, 13*(3), 6–8.

Christensen, K. (2009, August). *The three Rs of coaching.* Keynote address at the Pinellas County Schools Coaching Academy, St. Petersburg, FL.

Ciardiello, A. V. (2003). To wander and wonder: Pathways to literacy and inquiry through question finding. *Journal of Adolescent and Adult Literacy, 228–239.*

Cochran-Smith, M., & Lytle, S. L. (1993). *Inside/outside: Teacher research and knowledge.* New York: Teachers College Press.

Cochran-Smith, M., & Lytle, S. L. (1999). The teacher research movement: A decade later. *Educational Researcher, 28*(7), 15–25.

Cochran-Smith, M., & Lytle, S. L. (2001). Beyond certainty: Taking an inquiry stance on practice. In A. Lieberman & L. Miller (Eds.), *Teachers caught in the action: Professional development that matters* (pp. 45–58). New York: Teachers College Press.

Cochran-Smith, M., & Lytle, S. L. (2006). Troubling images of teaching in No Child Left Behind. *Harvard Educational Review, 76*(4), 668–697.

Cochran-Smith, M., & Lytle, S. L. (2009). *Inquiry as stance: Practitioner research for the next generation.* New York: Teachers College Press.

Copland, M. A. (2003). Leadership of inquiry: Building and sustaining capacity for school improvement. *Educational Evaluation and Policy Analysis, 25*(4), 375–395.

Cox, M. D. (2004). Introduction to faculty learning communities. *New Directions for Teaching and Learning, 97,* 5–23.

Cushman, K. (1999). *The cycle of inquiry and action: Essential learning communities.* Oakland, CA: Coalition of Essential Schools. Retrieved November 30, 2010, from http://www.essentialschools.org/resources/72

Dana, N. F. (2009). *Leading with passion and knowledge: The principal as action researcher.* Thousand Oaks, CA: Corwin.

Dana, N. F., Silva, D. Y., & Snow-Gerono, J. (2002). Building a culture of inquiry in professional development schools. *Teacher Education and Practice, 15*(4), 71–89.

Dana, N. F., Tricarico, K., & Quinn, D. (2010). The administrator as action researcher: A case study of five principals and their engagement in systematic, intentional study of their own practice. *Journal of School Leadership, 19*(3), 232–265.

Dana, N. F., & Yendol-Hoppey, D. (2008). *The reflective educator's guide to professional development: Coaching inquiry-oriented learning communities.* Thousand Oaks, CA: Corwin.

Dana, N. F., & Yendol-Hoppey, D. (2009). *The reflective educator's guide to classroom research: Learning to teach and teaching to learn through practitioner inquiry.* Thousand Oaks, CA: Corwin.

Darling-Hammond, L. (1994). Developing professional development schools: Early lessons, challenge, and promise. In L. Darling-Hammond (Ed.), *Professional development schools: Schools for developing a profession* (pp. 1–27). New York: Teachers College Press.

Darling-Hammond, L. (1999). *Teacher quality and student achievement: A review of state policy evidence.* Seattle: University of Washington, Center for the Study of Teaching and Policy.

Darling-Hammond, L., Barron, B., Pearson, P. D., Schoenfeld, A. H., Stage, E. K., Zimmerman, T. D. . . . Tilson, J. L. (2008). *Powerful learning: What we know about teaching for understanding.* San Francisco: Jossey-Bass.

Darling-Hammond, L., & McLaughlin, M. W. (1995). Policies that support professional development in an era of reform. *Phi Delta Kappan, 76*(8), 597–604.

Davenport, T. H. (2005). *Thinking for a living: How to get better performance and results from knowledge workers.* Boston: Harvard Business School Press.

Desimone, L. M. (2009). Improving impact studies of teachers' professional development: Toward better conceptualizations and measures. *Educational Researcher, 38,* 181–199.

Downey, C. J., Steffy, B. E., English, F. W., Frase, L. E., & Poston, W. K. (2004). *The three-minute classroom walk-through: Changing school supervisory practice one teacher at a time.* Thousand Oaks, CA: Corwin.

Drexler, W. (2010a). *The networked student: A design-based research case study of student constructed personal learning environments in a middle school science course.* Unpublished doctoral dissertation, The University of Florida, Gainesville.

Drexler, W. (2010b). The networked student model for construction of personal learning environments: Balancing teacher control and student autonomy. *Australasian Journal of Educational Technology, 26*(3), 369–385.

DuFour, R. (2004). What is a "professional learning community"? *Educational Leadership, 61*(8), 6–11.

Easton, L. B. (2004). *Powerful designs for professional learning.* Oxford, OH: National Staff Development Council.

Edwards, C. H. (1997). Promoting student inquiry. *The Science Teacher, 64*(7), 18–21.

Edwards, C. H. (2004). *Teaching and learning in middle and secondary schools: Student empowerment through learning communities.* Upper Saddle River, NJ: Prentice Hall.

Flinder, D. J. (1988). Teacher isolation and the new reform. *Journal of Curriculum and Supervision, 4*(1), 17–29.

Garmston, R. J. (2007). Results-oriented agendas transform meetings into valuable collaborative events. *Journal of Staff Development Council, 28*(2), 55–56.

Hall, T. (2002). *Differentiated instruction.* Wakefield, MA: National Center on Accessing the General Curriculum. Retrieved November 11, 2008, from http://www.cast.org/publications/ncac/ncac_diffinstruc.html

Hubbard, R. S., & Power, B. M. (1999). *Living the questions: A guide for teacher researchers.* York, ME: Stenhouse.

Hunter, D., Bailey, A., & Taylor, B. (1995). *The zen of groups: A handbook for people meeting with a purpose.* Marana, AZ: Fisher Books.

International Society for Technology in Education. (2007). *ISTE national educational technology standards (NETS_S) and performance indicators for students.* Retrieved August 10, 2009, from http://www.iste.org/standards.aspx

Joyce, B. R., & Showers, B. (1995). *Student achievement through staff development.* White Plains, NY: Longman.

Killion, J. (2009). Coaches' roles, responsibilities, and reach. In J. Knight (Ed.), *Coaching approaches and perspectives* (pp. 7–28). Thousand Oaks, CA: Corwin.

Killion, J., & Harrison, C. (2006). *Taking the lead: New roles for teachers and school-based coaches.* Oxford, OH: National Staff Development Council.

Knight, J. (2007). *Instructional coaching: A partnership approach to improving instruction.* Thousand Oaks, CA: Corwin.

Knight, J. (2011). *Unmistakable impact: A partnership approach for dramatically improving instruction.* Thousand Oaks, CA: Corwin.

Knowles, M. S. (1990). *The adult learner: A neglected species* (Rev. ed.). Houston, TX: Gulf.

Kur, J. (2000, April). *Dinosaurs in the primary classroom: From facts and crafts to inquiry.* Paper presented at the second annual State College Area School

District–Pennsylvania State University Teacher Inquiry Conference, State College, PA.

Kur, J., & Heitzmann, M. (2008). Attracting student wonderings: Magnets pull young students into scientific inquiry. *Science and Children, 45*(5), 28–32.

Levstik, L. S., & Barton, K. C. (2001). *Doing history: Investigating with children in elementary and middle schools.* Mahwah, NJ: Lawrence Erlbaum Associates.

Lewis, C., Perry, R., & Hurd, J. (2004). A deeper look at lesson study. *Educational Leadership, 61*(5), 18.

Lieberman, A., & Miller, L. (1990). Teacher development in professional practice schools. *Teachers College Record, 92*(1), 105–122.

Lieberman, A., & Miller, L. (1992). *Teachers—Their world and their work: Implications for school improvement.* New York: Teachers College Press.

Lortie, D. C. (1975). *Schoolteacher: A sociological study.* Chicago: University of Chicago Press.

Louis, K. S., & Marks, H. M. (1998). Does a professional learning community affect the classroom? Teachers work and student experiences in restructuring schools. *American Journal of Education, 106*, 532–575.

Luckie, D. B., Maleszewski, J. J., Loznak, S. D., & Krha, M. (2004). Infusion of collaborative inquiry throughout a biology curriculum increases student learning: A four-year study of "teams and streams." *Advances in Physiology Education, 28*(4), 199–209.

McDonald, J. P., Mohr, N., Dichter, A., & McDonald, E. C. (2003). *The power of protocols: An educator's guide to better practice.* New York: Teachers College Press.

Mezirow, J. (2000). Learning to think like an adult: Core concepts of transformational theory. In J. Mezirow & Associates (Eds.), *Learning as transformation: Critical perspectives on a theory in progress* (pp. 3–33). San Francisco: Jossey-Bass.

Militello, M., Rallis, S. F., & Goldring, E. B. (2009). *Leading with inquiry and action: How principals improve teaching and learning.* Thousand Oaks, CA: Corwin.

National Council for Accreditation of Teacher Education. (2010, November). *Transforming teacher education through clinical practice: A national strategy to prepare effective teachers.* Retrieved from http://www.ncate.org

National Research Council. (1996). *National science education standards.* Washington, DC: National Academy Press.

National Staff Development Council. (2009, May 16). *Professional development.* Retrieved June 12, 2009, from http://www.nsdc.org/standfor/definition.cfm

Partnership for 21st Century Skills. (2007). *Skills framework.* Route 21. Retrieved August 10, 2009, from http://www.21stcenturyskills.org/route21/

Pink, D. H. (2009). *Drive: The surprising truth about what motivates us.* New York: Penguin.

Putnam, R. (1995). Bowling alone: America's declining social capital. *Journal of Democracy, 6,*1.

Ross, D., Adams, A., Bondy, E., Dana, N. F., Dodman, S., & Packer, C. (2010, May). *Preparing teacher leaders: The impact of a cohort-based, job-embedded, blended teacher leadership program.* Paper presented at the annual meeting of the American Educational Research Association, Denver, CO.

Ross, D., Adams, A., Pape, S., Adams, T., Jacobbe, T., McArthur, K., & Pace, B. (2010). *Secrets of successful teaching: Lessons from award-winning teachers, 2008 and 2009.* Gainesville, FL: University of Florida, Lastinger Center Clearinghouse.

Ruddock, J., & Hopkins, D. (Eds.). (1985). *Research as a basis for teaching: Readings from the work of Lawrence Stenhouse.* London: Heinemann.

Saphier, J., & West, L. (2009 December). How coaches can maximize student learning. *Phi Delta Kappan, 91*(4), 46–50.

Schein, E. H. (2010). *Helping: How to offer, give, and receive help.* San Francisco: Berrett-Koehler.

Schmoker, M. (2004). The tipping point: From feckless reform to substantive instructional improvement. *Phi Delta Kappan, 85*(6), 424–432.

Schmoker, M. (2006). *Results now: How we can achieve unprecedented improvements in teaching and learning.* Alexandria, VA: Association for Supervision and Curriculum Development.

Senge, P. (2007). *Society for organizational learning.* Retrieved June 19, 2007, from http://www.solonline.org/pra/tool/skills.html

Smith, S. C., & Scott, J. J. (1990). *The collaborative school: A work environment for effective instruction.* Eugene, OR: ERIC Clearinghouse on Educational Management and the National Association of Secondary School Principals.

Steinberg, S. R., & Kincheloe, J. L. (1998). *Students as researchers: Creating classrooms that matter.* Bristol, PA: Falmer Press.

Stoicovy, D., Burns, R. W., Ciuffetelli, L., & Harris, P. (2009, March). *Turning learning inside out: Professional development in a PDS.* Paper presented at the annual meeting of the National Association of Professional Development Schools, Daytona Beach, FL.

Stonewater, J. K. (2005). Inquiry teaching and learning: The best math class study. *School Science and Mathematics, 105,* 36–47. Retrieved from http://findarticles .com/p/articles/mi_qa3667/is_200501/ai_n9467815/

Sweeney, D. (2010). *Student-centered coaching: A guide for K–8 coaches and principals.* Thousand Oaks, CA: Corwin.

Taylor, R. (2002, December). Shaping the culture of learning communities. *Principal Leadership, 3*(4), 42–45.

Tomlinson, C. A. (1999). *The differentiated classroom: Responding to the needs of all learners.* Alexandria, VA: ASCD.

Tomlinson, C. A. (2001). *How to differentiate instruction in mixed-ability classrooms* (2nd ed.) Alexandria, VA: ASCD.

Wagner, T. (2008). *The global achievement gap: Why even our best schools don't teach the new survival skills our children need—and what we can do about it.* New York: Basic Books.

Warren, M. R., Hong, S., Rubin, C. H., & Uy, P. S. (2009). Beyond the bake sale: A community-based relational approach to parent engagement in schools. *Teachers College Record, 111*(9), 2209–2254.

Wheatley, M. (2002). *Turning to one another: Simple conversations to restore hope to the future.* San Francisco: Berrett-Koshler.

Whitford, B. L., & Wood, D. R. (2010). Teachers learning in community: Realities and possibilities. Albany: State University of New York Press.

Wilhelm, J. D. (2007). *Engaging readers and writers with inquiry.* New York: Scholastic.

Wolk, S. (2008). School as inquiry. *Phi Delta Kappan, 90*(2), 115–122.

Wolkenhauer, R., Boynton, S., & Dana, N. F. (2011). *The power of practitioner research and development of an inquiry stance in teacher education programs.* Paper presented at the annual meeting of the Association of Teacher Educators, Orlando, FL.

Wright, J. (n.d.). *RTI_WIRE.* Retrieved from http://www.jimwrightonline.com/ php/rti/rti_wire.php

Yendol-Hoppey, D., & Dana, N. F. (2010). *Powerful professional development: Building expertise within the four walls of your school.* Thousand Oaks, CA: Corwin.

Index

CORWIN

A SAGE Company

The Corwin logo—a raven striding across an open book—represents the union of courage and learning. Corwin is committed to improving education for all learners by publishing books and other professional development resources for those serving the field of PreK–12 education. By providing practical, hands-on materials, Corwin continues to carry out the promise of its motto: **"Helping Educators Do Their Work Better."**

Advancing professional learning for student success

Learning Forward (formerly National Staff Development Council) is an international association of learning educators committed to one purpose in K–12 education: Every educator engages in effective professional learning every day so every student achieves.